LAND ACKNOWLEDGMENT

Chicago is part of the traditional homelands of the Council of the Three Fires: the Odawa, Ojibwe, and Potawatomi nations. Many other tribes—such as the Miami, Ho-Chunk, Sac, and Fox—also called this area home. Located at the intersection of several great waterways, the land naturally became a site of travel and healing for many tribes. Today, Chicago is still a place that calls people from diverse backgrounds to live and gather. American Indians continue to live in the region, and Chicago is home to the country's third-largest urban American Indian community, which still practices its heritage and traditions, including care for the land and waterways. Despite the numerous changes the city has experienced, its American Indian and architecture communities both see the importance of the land and of this place, which has always been hospitable to many different backgrounds and perspectives.

—American Indian Center of Chicago

...AND OTHER SUCH STORIES

...AND OTHER SUCH STORIES

EDITED BY
YESOMI UMOLU, SEPAKE ANGIAMA,
PAULO TAVARES

CHICAGO ARCHITECTURE BIENNIAL
IN ASSOCIATION WITH
COLUMBIA BOOKS ON ARCHITECTURE AND THE CITY

PREFACE

On behalf of the City of Chicago, I am honored to welcome visitors to the 2019 Chicago Architecture Biennial. My wife, Amy, and I are proud to be Honorary Co-Chairs of this landmark exhibition, which looks beyond specific styles and techniques to explore how architects and designers address broader social issues as they reimagine communities for the future. As the largest survey of contemporary architecture in North America, the Biennial positions Chicago at the center of international dialogue about the field's impact on urban life.

Chicago is a city rich in architectural history and innovation, and the Biennial has become an integral element of our expansive cultural offerings, featuring programming throughout Chicago, including symposiums on housing affordability, accessibility, and open space. I am especially enthusiastic about the ways the Biennial has embraced community arts centers, libraries, schools, and other neighborhood institutions. Through educational programs, the exhibition's themes have been extended into every area of our city, broadening the horizons of audiences of all ages and backgrounds.

I offer my sincere gratitude to all those whose financial commitments have made this event possible, including the local foundations, corporations, and individuals whose support contributes immeasurably to the cultural fabric of our city. That the Biennial is free and open to the public is a particularly fitting expression of Chicago hospitality—our way of saying welcome!

This publication extends that sense of openness and generosity by incorporating a variety of voices and perspectives, weaving reflections on this great city's past and future architectural legacy with the stories of regions around the world. I hope visitors to the Biennial and readers of this volume will find inspiration, as I do, in the ways creativity and innovation can transform the built environment we share.

Lori E. Lightfoot
Mayor of Chicago

FOREWORD

...and other such stories, the third edition of the Chicago Architecture Biennial (CAB), builds upon the evolutionary process by which we have come to understand the Biennial's legacy and mission since its inception in 2015. As an organization granted a civic charter in former mayor Rahm Emanuel's Chicago Cultural Plan 2012, we've been charged with advancing global ideas about architecture in ways that resonate locally. Together Graham Foundation Artistic Director Yesomi Umolu and Co-Curators Sepake Angiama and Paulo Tavares have centered the value that new narratives can play in this organization's imperative to foster fresh thinking about issues in architecture and the built environment more broadly. Our curators have foregrounded the notion that the most resilient stores of cultural knowledge reside in the body of stories we hold in common.

The questions posed by the curatorial team's focus and explored by contributors to *...and other such stories* connect to a wider public and are further amplified through the Biennial's extensive partnership platform, which engages more than one hundred organizations from this city and the world beyond, with the city of Chicago serving as host and convener.

The cumulative conversations and pedagogical exchanges undertaken by our exhibition contributors and program partners will once again reach hundreds of thousands of individuals, including the thousands of young people who will participate in CAB's Learning Initiatives. Together this collective public—galvanized by new ideas and approaches, modeling new relations and new actions, and discovering allies from distant geographies—has enormous transformative potential. In the face of entrenched but shared global challenges that have, in so many ways, been "learned," we take inspiration from the possibility that the inequities of the world we live in might, through the concerted efforts of this broader public, be unlearned and dismantled.

Essential to the task of connecting this energizing set of conversations from which societies can learn to see anew is the Biennial staff and the extensive creative team. Through diligent and passionate teamwork they have once again ensured that in 2019 the exhibition and curatorial program anchor this broader platform by which we reach a larger world. We are also grateful to our co-publishing partner, Columbia Books on Architecture and the City, for believing and investing in this project with us.

As the Biennial looks ahead to how we build on the impact of this edition in 2021 and beyond, we envision working deliberately and collaboratively with grassroots partners; allies in architecture, culture, and aligned fields; and the city's leadership (including Mayor Lori Lightfoot and First Lady Amy Eshleman, the Honorary Co-Chairs of CAB) to steward these conversations toward transformational goals. We envision shifting dynamics of power, exerting new collective will, working collaboratively across geographies, and shaping new approaches to and policies for the built environment.

Todd Palmer
Executive Director
Chicago Architecture Biennial

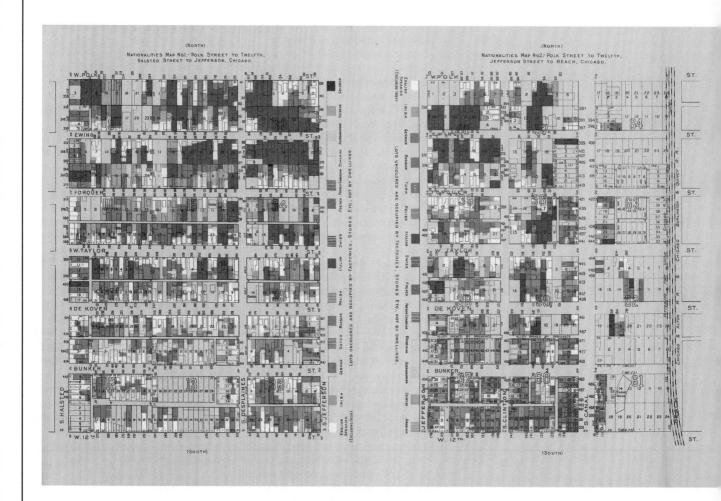

Nationalities Maps from Hull-House Maps and Papers, 1895. Courtesy Cornell University—PJ Mode Collection of Persuasive Cartography

Lori Lightfoot, Chicago's newly installed mayor, the first African American and openly gay woman to hold the office, declared in a post on Twitter on June 21, 2019, "Chicago will always be a welcoming city and a champion for the rights of our immigrant and refugee communities." Just a little over a month after she became mayor, Lightfoot publicly refused to assist a federal order to seize and deport undocumented residents, bringing the city of Chicago back to its beginnings as a sanctuary for immigrants and migrants. Jane Addams and Ellen Gates Starr founded the Hull-House settlement

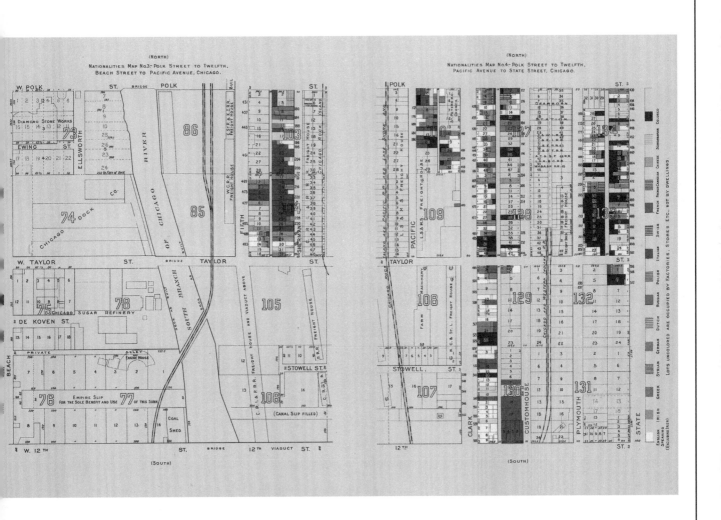

Nationalities Map No.3- Polk Street to Twelfth, Beach Street to Pacific Avenue, Chicago.

Nationalities Map No.4- Polk Street to Twelfth, Pacific Avenue to State Street, Chicago.

in 1889, intentionally placing it in Chicago's most diverse immigrant neighborhood. Determined to fight xenophobia, expose the root causes of poverty, and break down class boundaries, these visionary social reformers conducted an unprecedented neighborhood sociological study. They went door-to-door, asked residents about their daily lives, compiled information, and analyzed conditions of different ethnic groups living on the West Side. They included color-coded maps outlining the ethnicities and family income of residents. Hull-House reformers went on to use the data, maps, and essays to help pass laws in support of fair housing, to close sweatshops, to advocate for more services for the community, and to address other social inequities.
—Jennifer Scott

THE CITY OTHERWISE

YESOMI UMOLU
SEPAKE ANGIAMA
PAULO TAVARES

BETWEEN LAND AND SKY

Looking back at our research process for the third edition of the Chicago Architecture Biennial, we are reminded of a walk in Vancouver led by Herb Varley (Nisga'a/Mowachaht) in early 2019. Guiding us through the rapidly gentrifying Downtown Eastside neighborhood, Herb introduced us to the complexities of urban life for marginalized communities struggling to find safe spaces for shelter. Among Herb's many thought-provoking statements that day was his acknowledgment that Vancouver should be deemed an illegal occupation. Indeed, the city was established on traditional territories of the Musqueam, Squamish, and Tsleil-Waututh First Nations that were never transferred to incoming European settlers, whether by war, treaty, commercial exchange, or gift.[1] For Herb and local housing rights activists, recognizing this fact allows a rethinking of the terms of land ownership and occupation, connecting present-day evictions in rapidly gentrifying downtown Vancouver to the historical displacements of settler-colonialism.[2]

It is possible to extrapolate beyond the shores of Vancouver and consider other global cities as sites of ongoing processes of colonial occupation and expansion, thereby opening new ways of understanding conflicts over land, public space, housing, and civic representation. These issues are not exclusively the product of past regimes. As we witnessed in Vancouver—and elsewhere during our research[3]—Indigenous communities continue to struggle for land and sovereignty. And in many

Fig. 1
Gentrification walking tour of Vancouver with Herb Varley, 2019.
Photo: Dennis Ha

1.
In 2014 the city of Vancouver officially acknowledged that it is on unceded Aboriginal territory. Colin Schultz, "One of Canada's Biggest Cities Just Acknowledged That It Was Built on Unceded Aboriginal Territory," *Smithsonian*, June 26, 2014, www.smithsonianmag.com/smart-news/one-canadas-biggest-cities-just-officially-admitted-it-was-built-unceded-aboriginal-territory-180951873/.

2.
For further discussion of the debates surrounding land rights and sovereignty in Vancouver, see the interview between Sepake Angiama, Vincent Tao, and cheyanne turions on pages 111–15 in this volume.

3.
In São Paulo we learned of the Guarani Indigenous community's struggle to reclaim ancestral lands and sacred sites in the city.

4.
Luxury condominiums and other high-end real estate developments often remain vacant, acting as financial assets without social function. Ryan Holmes, "Without Affordable Housing, Vancouver Risks Becoming an Economic Ghost Town," *Financial Times*, business.financialpost.com/entrepreneur/fp-startups/without-affordable-housing-vancouver-risks-becoming-an-economic-ghost-town.

5.
For further discussion of MSTC's work, see the conversation between Paulo Tavares and Carmen Silva on pages 33–39 in this volume.

cities today these challenges extend to other groups whose rights to affordable housing are being threatened by vast swaths of high-end real estate development—Vancouver, for example, is one of many locations afflicted by increasing rates of absentee ownership.[4]

Architecture and planning play important roles here. Buildings and urban infrastructure have become material symbols of capital investment and are often used as tools for enacting displacements on the ground. In this new, transactional paradigm we are told that speculators, developers, and investors reign supreme. But in what ways can rethinking the terms of ownership and occupancy provide improved spatial conditions for the landless and the roofless? How can architecture and planning be rearticulated toward the common good?

ANY GIVEN SPACE

Answers to these questions can be found in the words of Carmen Silva, leader of Movimento Sem Teto do Centro (MSTC, City Center Homeless People's Movement) in São Paulo.[5] Speaking to a group convened during our visit to the city in fall 2018, Carmen emphasized the importance of MSTC's advocacy for working-class families and individuals, including migrants and refugees from around Latin America, Africa, and the Middle East.[6] She also shared MSTC's vision for more diverse and inclusive cities in which social movements are active agents in urban planning.

For Carmen, MSTC's repurposing of vacant buildings in the city center to benefit thousands of families does not constitute illegal occupation but is rather an act of care that directly supports the fundamental human right to shelter and access to the work, culture, and education opportunities that lead to socioeconomic security in metropolitan areas. The movement's stewardship of vacant buildings reflects a deep appreciation of the social function of the built environment, proposing the use and habitation of space in ways that extend beyond market-driven forces. Such a powerful vision of "urban renewal" is not based on the top-down, financially intensive processes that architecture often serves today but instead on new forms of civic agency and social solidarity.

The lack of affordable housing in Vancouver and São Paulo—whether for local, migrant, or refugee residents—mirrors that in London, a city that witnessed a social housing boom in the 1960s and 1970s but now finds itself facing a severe housing crisis due to neoliberal policies implemented in recent decades. Other world cities, such as Mumbai, struggle to keep pace with the residential development required to house their rapidly growing populations, a challenge that represents another facet of this crisis, which today affects virtually every metropolis, north and south.

We have often found that the problems cities face are less related to scarcity of space than to a failing of will and policy in city government to make safe and affordable housing universally available. The case of the Grenfell Tower fire in London,[7] which cast a long shadow over our research trajectory, speaks directly to the bitter consequences of such

Fig. 2
Grenfell Tower after the fire, London, 2017. Photo: Carl Court / Getty Images

Fig. 3
Preparing for the removal of the statue of Cecil Rhodes, University of Cape Town, South Africa, 2015. Photo: Nic Bothma / EPA / Shutterstock

neglect. So how can communities confronted with such realities mobilize their voices and advocate for their rights to the city? And how might the profession of architecture build into its methodologies and the life cycles of its buildings the possibility of advocacy as a spatial practice?

ARCHITECTURES OF ERASURE

In Johannesburg we met with scholars, architects, and activists involved in reshaping definitions of public space in post-apartheid South Africa. Here our conversations addressed occupation as the illegal attainment of land by colonial and apartheid regimes, the vestiges of which populate public spaces across the nation. We also discussed how engaging with these spatial legacies can be an act of resistance, one often played out through architecture. For the many students who took part in the protests that erupted around a call to remove a monument dedicated to British colonialist Cecil Rhodes at the University of Cape Town, it was a question of decolonizing public histories, spaces, institutions, and educational systems, and thereby removing oppressive forces from the country's present and future.[8]

An empty plinth in a public square raises curiosity. What stood there before, and what is to come in its place? At a time when insurgent political bodies and collective subjectivities are emerging to challenge hegemonic narratives of oppression and power, many monuments and memorials honoring repressive ideologies have fallen. As Paulo wrote in a group chat on WhatsApp after facing the

6.
This resonates with the occupation in Athens of City Plaza, a hotel building that was abandoned during the financial crisis of 2008 and later converted into an autonomous housing center for Greek workers and non-European migrants and refugees. In her essay on pages 135–40 of this volume, Pelin Tan describes the ways in which this context of shared precariousness gives rise to forms of commoning that challenge established definitions of citizenship based on national borders.

7.
In 2017 a fire ravaged this twenty-four-story, block-long building in the center of London, causing seventy-two deaths. The cause of the fire and the response by local authorities prompted national debate around the decline of social housing provisions and issues of negligence and lack of accountability within the building industry and city government.

8.
See the interview between Yesomi Umolu, Inam Kula, and Aviwe Mandyanda on pages 75–80 of this volume.

remains of a Confederate monument in New Orleans: "This empty column, this ghost presence, there is something to it, in thinking about memory, city, and architecture." In such voids we see the renegotiation of histories and the contestation of architectures that keep *others* out.

The ways in which architecture and planning mediate time and memory is not the sole concern of public monuments. As our cities evolve, block by block, building by building, a process of accretion is enacted that simultaneously adds and removes. Only through excavation—whether material or conceptual—can we understand the depth of architecture's erasures. So how might architecture address spatial injustices, reframing (in)visibilities and historic narratives? Can architecture be conceived of as a discipline that extends beyond finite built forms, an ever-evolving practice concerned with the constant making and remaking of social space?

CITY IN A GARDEN

Chicago. This city's dizzying confluence of natural and human-made terrain owes its development to the extraction economies that transformed vast areas of the Great Plains into dense urban sprawl. Beyond Chicago, the American Midwest is home to equally dense networks of high-tech industrial plantations. A meeting point of numerous Indigenous communities, this region was once a complex ecological system of prairies, forests, and grasslands. Only the great Lake Michigan has eluded exploitation and erasure by the pervasive and destructive forces of westward expansion.

To consider the vastness of this body of water and the contributions it has made to sustaining America's industry and economic growth is to contend with our inextricable connection to and reliance on the natural world—an interdependence that is increasingly imperiled by capitalism's devastating effects on the planet's climatic balance.

On the not-too-distant horizon, the contemporary landscape of extraction threatens to extend its borders to the least exploited, best preserved ecosystems across the planet, reaching the depths of rain forests and the ocean seabed and conquering the last Indigenous territories on Earth. New forms of extractive capitalism are counteracted by new networks of transnational, anti-colonial resistance. Conflicts over land and nature, such as those sparked by the Dakota Access Pipeline and the BP oil spill in the Gulf of Mexico, or the mining dam collapses seen in Brazil between 2015 and 2019—to name just a few cases addressed in this Biennial—are paradigmatic of conditions across the world's most vulnerable and ecologically rich hinterlands.

Hearing from activists and members of Indigenous communities who stand at the front lines of these struggles has prompted us to reconsider conventional relationships between city, land, and nature. During our research we became attuned to the ways in which such voices are forging definitions of the social that expand beyond the human to other forms of life. Indeed, this publication opens with a land acknowledgment written by the American Indian Center (AIC) in Chicago, a text meant to

Fig. 4
Protests at Standing Rock Sioux Reservation over the Dakota Pipeline Access Project, North Dakota, 2016. Photo: Scott Olson / Getty Images

propose, as AIC director Heather Davis has written, "a call to rethink one's own relationship with the environment and the histories of all peoples." In Ecuador, for example, as Eduardo Kohn discusses in this volume, there are calls to establish a law of the living forest and to assert the rights of nature. The urgency to define new vocabularies, new laws, and new ethics of cohabitation and cultivation—to forge another "civic contract" between humans and other beings—is especially profound today as the climate and natural ecosystems strain under the weight of human intervention.

Within the city proper we are also witnessing new forms of activism that expand the notion of the civic to natural environments. In São Paulo we gathered under the open-air roof of the Teatro Oficina, designed by Lina Bo Bardi, an architect known for her recognition of Indigenous, Afro-Brazilian, and folk histories and traditions as well as for her sensitivity to the relationship between nature and the built environment. Bo Bardi's theater offers a master class in cooperative living across human and nonhuman communities. It is a place where elements of the natural world—trees, water, sun, wind, vegetation, and soil—intersect with the day-to-day activities of performers and audiences.

Here we listened as members of the theater company spoke about the building's inextricable connection to its context and community and the threat it faces as urban development encroaches. For them, the building should not be defined simply by its enclosure but rather by the lives contained within and around it. Their strategy to confront gentrification includes constructing a park instead of condominiums, a move that would revitalize not only the social space in the city but also the waterways, trees, fauna, and surrounding land.

How can architecture and urban planning frame the social as a sphere populated by multi-species networks and constituencies? In a time of climate emergency, can these disciplines reclaim the specificity of place and address our ongoing ecological crises through more effective means than those offered by the technocratic paradigm of "sustainability," claiming space for design that pushes beyond an anthropocentric lens?

...AND OTHER SUCH STORIES

We offer these stories and others throughout the Biennial and this publication in the interest of bringing together a multiplicity of perspectives on some of the most vital issues affecting our communities, metropolitan areas, and environments. In the course of making the Biennial, such stories have given us many insights on the relationships between the land, nature, and rights to the city; the political reality and imaginary of memory; and the socio-ecological impacts of urbanization and its attendant economies of extraction. We have addressed the use of architecture as a colonial tool for the building and unbuilding of cities and nations. And we have learned that creation and destruction are always political, as even absence evokes a haunting presence.

Our work has taken us to various locations around the world, but our start and end point has always been Chicago. We have confronted the city's history as a colonial settlement established through war, displacement, and other brutalities. Marked by the disavowal of rights to occupancy for Native Americans and, subsequently, African American communities, Chicago's history is characterized by an impulse to divide and conquer. Yet it has also come to be known as "the city of neighborhoods," and this legacy, too, has generated many stories. Chicago is a place of incredible social and cultural diversity, and its urban fabric has been molded by some of the most progressive forms of collective solidarity and civic engagement, making it a landmark site in the history of the labor and civil rights movements in America. Looking at Chicago today, we understand that its fraught and fascinating history continues to inflect its complex present. Our work, for the Biennial and in this volume, is to trace stories that originate from this place but resonate in geographies elsewhere, revealing dialogues between various practices across the world and surfacing questions that connect many communities, cities, territories, and ecologies today.

At the heart of it all is the Chicago Cultural Center, the city's first public library, nestled along busy Michigan Avenue. The 2019 Biennial *occupies* this building as a place in which to gather, to think from, and to interrogate what makes the city today. In this space we begin our consideration of who (or what) has the agency to imagine the city differently and by what means it can be transformed, as well as of how the city might produce, publish, preserve, circulate, and perform those narratives. This gesture is extended across neighborhoods through a series of collaborations with Chicago-based organizations and communities aimed at fostering conversations that resonate simultaneously at a local and global scale. Mirroring the archival impulse and storytelling capacities of the library—and the city as repository—this publication deploys historical and contemporary records alongside essays and interviews to draw out multiple perspectives and positions. Taken together, *...and other such stories* opens up arenas of speculation that imagine the built and natural environments in more inclusive and diverse ways, projecting an image of the city otherwise.

CHAPTER 1

RIGHTS AND RECLAMATIONS

Casa Aztlán, Chicago, 2017. Photo: Sebastián Hidalgo

In June 2017 the murals that once surrounded the entrance to Casa Aztlán, one of the oldest Mexican American community centers in Chicago, were covered in gray paint as developers prepared to convert the space into a luxury apartment building. Community members and activists gathered outside the Casa—the Spanish word for "house"—to mourn and protest this act of erasure, one of many signs of the ongoing process of urban gentrification and displacement occuring in the historic Mexican American neighborhood of Pilsen.

THE RACIAL QUESTION(ING) OF JUSTICE

DENISE FERREIRA DA SILVA

"This ... is called a rubber bullet, it hurts when it hits the body," says Cláudio dos Santos. He refers to the action of the military police (MP) of the metropolitan civil guard in Comunidade do Cimento, in the eastern zone of São Paulo (SP), which burned Saturday night. [São Paulo, 2019]

[Jessica] Patrick was a member of the Lake Babine First Nation and had a young daughter....

Johansen received confirmation from a family member about Patrick's death Saturday night, and asked the family for permission to conduct a vigil, which included a drumming ceremony, in Patrick's honour.

About 200 people gathered at Bovill Square Sunday afternoon. Many attendees wore red as a reminder of the national issue of missing and murdered indigenous women, which includes 18 murders and disappearances along the so-called Highway of Tears, the stretch of Hwy. 16 between Prince George and Prince Rupert that goes through Smithers, since the 1970s. [Smithers, British Columbia, 2018]

"Yes there was taunting of the police. We were telling them to go."

A tear gas cannister was lobbed into the crowd as another school group approached and children started scattering in all directions.

The policemen—mostly black—got back into their vehicles, which were stoned. "Their only way out was to drive through the crowd."

Morobe said what struck him was that most of the policemen at the scene were black, "pointing guns at their own children," and that the commanding officer was white.

"That crowd of policemen still have something to explain," he said. [Soweto, 1976]

Two colored men are reported to have been killed and approximately fifty whites and negroes injured, a number probably fatally, in race riots that broke out at south side beaches yesterday. The rioting spread through the black belt and by midnight had thrown the entire south side into a state of turmoil....

One Negro was knocked off a raft at the Twenty-ninth street beach after he had been stoned by whites. He drowned because whites are said to have frustrated attempts of colored bathers to rescue him....

A colored rioter is said to have died from wounds inflicted by Policeman John O'Brien, who

Epigraphs:
"Incêndio destrói ocupação em São Paulo (SP) horas antes da reintegração de posse," *Brasil de Fato*, March 24, 2019, www.brasildefato .com.br/2019/03/24 /incendio-destroi -ocupacao-em-sao-paulo -sp-horas-antes-da -reintegracao-de-posse /; Cheryl Chan, "Vigil Held for 18-year-old Smithers Woman after Human Remains Found," *Vancouver Sun*, September 17, 2018, https://vancouversun. com/news/local-news/ vigil-held-for-18-year-old- smithers-woman-after- human-remains-found; South African Press Association, "Policemen Involved in June 16 Shootings Have to Explain: Morobe," news release, July 23, 1996, www.justice .gov.za/trc/media %5C1996%5C9607 /s960723k.htm; "'A Crowd of Howling Negroes': The Chicago Daily Tribune Reports the Chicago Race Riot, 1919," History Matters, historymatters .gmu.edu/d/4975/.

1.
Marilla Brocchetto and Nicole Chavez, "Protests Break Out in Chicago after Man Is Fatally Shot," CNN, July 15, 2018, www.cnn.com/2018/07/14 /us/chicago-officer -involved-shooting/index .html.

2.
Marilla Brocchetto and Nicole Chavez, "Protesters Disrupt Chicago Shops, Ask Feds to Probe McDonald Killing," CNN, November 28, 2015, www.cnn.com /2015/11/27/us/chicago -protests-laquan -mcdonald/index.html.

fired into a mob at Twenty-ninth street and Cottage Grove avenue. [Chicago, 1919]

Echoing demands for justice for Jessica Patrick and other murdered and disappeared First Nations women from British Columbia, for residents of Chicago's "Black Belt," for Soweto's schoolchildren, and for those who lost everything in a fire in an occupation in São Paulo, protesters on the streets of Chicago ask, "Who do you protect? Who do you serve?"[1] The question of justice echoes the cries of mothers, fathers, siblings, relatives, neighbors, ancestors and descendants, friends, and relations, resonating in each and every particle of each and every inch of air and water, and on land in buildings, streets, cars, beaches, bicycles, squirrels, dogs, racoons, even the cries of coyotes, salmon, and trees. Everything, every tiny little bit of matter, echoes cries heard and unheard. Though there is not much more left to do than to ask the question, it does not present itself unmediated. When colonial and racial violence is attended to, taken into account, in the description of the scene of the killing, the where and when it happens, it removes justice from where it has been located for the past two hundred years or so. Colonial and racial violence is authorized by the modern juridical apparatus—that is, the structures and mechanisms of law enforcement and administration of justice—which protects settlers and citizens.

When the demand for justice echoes its failures, it suspends the political question because it extracts from it the principles (equality and sovereignty) that have sustained the reign of the transparent subject, and its polities, since its articulation about two hundred years ago. It recalls how racial violence refigures colonial violence in the city space and, in doing so, dissolves the temporal separation of "native" and "slave" from Indigenous and black collectives, past and present expropriation, and old and new forms of extraction. When the racial question is raised to justice, it is nothing short of a questioning of demands for redress articulated from the confines of the existing political text. The racial question renders decolonization the horizon of justice.

Taste the air, the nanoparticles, and you might sense the steps of Jean Baptiste Point du Sable and his wife, Kitihawa, as they walked on the farm at the mouth of the Chicago River, just before this black settler, his Potawatomi wife, and their descendants left, mostly likely anticipating that they would not fare well as the white (British, French, and American) settlers attempted to establish control of the Illiniwek, Miami, and Potawatomi, to name a few of the Indigenous peoples of these lands. Listen and hear the cries before the killing in 1919 of young and old African Americans who had moved to Chicago, fleeing Jim Crow and lynching in the South and hoping to take over the industrial and other jobs vacated by white workers fighting in the dreadful war. Touch the cries of those who revolted after the news of the assassination of Martin Luther King Jr. and its threat to the promise of racial equality embodied in the civil rights gains of the previous

Fig. 1
Protesters demonstrate in response to the fatal shooting of Laquan McDonald, Chicago, 2015. Photo: Andrew Nelles / Reuters

Fig. 2
Police after firing bullets at residents at a service delivery protest, Pennyville, Johannesburg, 2019. Photo: Nhlanhla Phillips / African News Agency

years. If one breathes deeply, the sounds of each of the sixteen bullets that hit Lacquan McDonald's body in October 2014 can be heard.[2] Listening, tasting, touching, smelling might make it possible to see justice in its failings. Lurking behind just about every explanation, every justification, for police killings and the courts' failure to prosecute the murderers of Indigenous and black persons in the United States, Canada, Brazil, and elsewhere, the racial question awaits attention.

How is the question to be asked? How is it to be formulated if each and every racial event belies how time and its referents (interiority and historicity) provide no context for redress and if space's primary function in modern thinking has always been to assign the limits of time? Asking these questions—which in reality are one and the same question—in a reflection on architectural practices, I am obviously recalling (but not necessarily claiming) the city's juridical (*civitas*) and ethical (*communitas*) significance. Because the question in need of formulation, the one for which this is a preface and an outline, carries in itself the very questioning of justice, or better, it asks the question *about* justice, which it presents as what becomes of redress if it is to address colonial violence. When considered from here, from how "natives" and "slaves" and their descendants inhabit the modern ethico-juridical framework, justice becomes something *spatiotemporally*—that is *racially*—delimited. When considered from here, from where racial violence rules, it is impossible to ignore how the city's

Fig. 3
Marchers protest the killing of councilwoman and human rights activist Marielle Franco and her driver, Anderson Pedro Gomes, Rio de Janeiro, 2018. Photo: Leo Correa / Associated Press.

Fig. 4
Three women stand vigil on October 4 on Parliament Hill during the annual commemoration of the missing and murdered Indigenous women of Canada, also known as Stolen Sisters, Ottawa, 2012. Courtesy Susanne Ure

ethico-juridical apparatus refigures both the polity (in its administrative policies) and the colony (in its law enforcement practices).

How then can the racial question become a proper ethical and political question? A few changes have to be made in our thinking about how we exist in the world. An important one is in how we *make sense* of what has happened, what is happening, and what may come to happen as deeply implicated. Among other things, that requires dispensing with approaching the world as something to be apprehended and then comprehended as a web of causal chains that humans alone are able to understand. This is necessary because insofar as it is founded on an ethical program guided by the notion of the human, the current formulation of the political presupposes a certain conception of the events and the existent as comprehensible only if temporally (historically) and spatially (physically) limited—that is, finite. On the one hand, it renders what has happened separate from what is happening, unless they are placed in a causal chain—that is, as long as what happens is a consequence of what happened before. On the other hand, what exists has a presumed continuity within itself but only if it remains attached to itself in spite of the discontinuities of its environs. According to this mode of thinking, the racial question is immaterial—it does not matter—both because of the presumed temporal (historical) discontinuity between the colony and the polity as modes of governance and because of the presumed spatial (geographic) discontinuity

3.
By total violence, I mean the work of the colonial modality of power: the expropriation of land, labor, and life.

4.
V. I. Lenin, "Draft Theses on the Colonial and the National Question for the Second Congress of the Communist International," 1920, www.marxists.org /archive/lenin/works /1920/jun/05.htm.

5.
My references here are Lenin's as well as Stalin's, Ho Chi Minh's, Joseph Allen's, and C. L. R. James's writings on the colonial, national, and "Negro" questions. See especially Ho Chi Minh, "Some Considerations on the Colonial Question," www.marxists.org /reference/archive /ho-chi-minh/works /1922/05/25.htm; Joseph Allen, *The Negro Question in the United States* (New York: International Publishers, 1936); and C. L. R. James, *On the Negro Question* (Jackson: University of Mississippi Press, 1996).

6.
The same issue appears today in Alain Badiou's and Slavoj Žižek's statements on cultural difference, which I discuss in Denise Ferreira da Silva, "Fractal Thinking," *ACCeSsions*, no. 2 (April 27, 2016), accessions.org /article2/fractal -thinking/.

between the colonial subaltern (the native and the slave) and the political subaltern (the migrant and the refugee). For the black and Indigenous populations of the cities of Chicago, São Paulo, Johannesburg, and Vancouver, this spatial distinction disappears at every encounter with law enforcement, every time the courts fail to find officers guilty in acts of total violence.[3]

How much this presumption of separability hinders the very formulation of a properly modern political question—that is, one that addresses colonial and racial subjugation—is dramatically exemplified in classical Marxist thinkers' attempts to revise the historical-materialist project in light of an international context that expands beyond the boundaries of Europe to include the former colonies of the Americas and the new colonies of Africa and Asia. For Lenin, in 1905, the colonial question had the same status as a "problem" as did Ireland, the struggle against pan-Islamism, and "Negroes in America." All fell under the "problem of equality," whether it was posed by individuals (even if affected as groups, such as "the Negroes," or nationalities, such as the Poles in Russia).[4] For early twentieth-century Marxist thinkers, it seems, the national question encompassed everything racial as the latter was inclusive of the Caucasians in Russia and blacks in the United States. Further, they were but different presentations of the same issue—namely, how the proletarian revolution was to deal with the divisions caused by segregation and discrimination or whether and how it could take advantage of these groups as they organized to demand equality and autonomy.

For Marxism, in its various currents, the racial question was part of the general issue of divisiveness, and it had to be properly presented and addressed as an aspect of the revolution that only the proletariat could lead. For instance, the demand for "cultural-national autonomy" had been harmful in Russia and Austria, as it was divisive of the working class, leading to separatism: demarcation and segregation.[5] The setup is well known to us today, namely, how to deal with the particular nature of the national claim and the universal character of the proletariat aim and the international nature of its existence.[6] Nor had the racial question a proper place in the political imaginary that animated several lines of the critical political discourse of local and national struggles—communist, socialist, antiracist, feminist, LGBTQI—that is, the whole gamut of political movements that consolidated in the 1980s. These movements for social justice addressed the state under the assumption that it had the right to exist, that all that was needed was that the state include the rest of us, namely, the poor, black, Indigenous, female, gay folks. It is not that colonization (conquest and slavery) has not been part of that political vocabulary. It has been. However, the presentation of the racial question in the register of the colony—that is, as a cry against colonial domination—has been avoided because of how it immediately and instantaneously challenges what these political movements want to accomplish by being heard by the state.

For the descendants of the "native" and the "slave," those whose cries expose justice's failures, the racial-political question is inflected by colonial and racial violence. The way black and Indigenous peoples inhabit the cityscape today, to be sure, is not that different from how they inhabit the countryside. Neither the white farmer (in the Canadian prairies) nor the police officer (in the Brazilian favela) fears punishment precisely because the civil and human rights of the young or old Indigenous or black persons disappear in the ethical vortex that raciality institutes in the post-Enlightenment political discourse. This ethical vortex swallows the political question. It does so because as a figuring of the colonial in the symbolic register, raciality resolves the total violence that defines the colony into a moral deficit of (first) the racial subaltern and (second) the white person whose mind is not yet fully (but in time will be) occupied by universal reason.

Always postponed when the racial question surfaces, what is to come comes to mind later: after the critique of capital, after racial inclusion, after ... but it rarely does. Yet it has never been irrelevant. For what makes the question relevant is precisely what delays it: the racial question requires a description of the juridical and ethical context of confrontation that is not properly political or that is not the modern polity, which is the ethico-juridical arrangement distinct from the colony. A political formulation of the racial question requires a description of the context of confrontation that both takes into account and dissipates the distinction between the colony and the polity, the frontier and the city. In the Americas it requires a point of departure that begins and stays with total violence—conquest and slavery— and proceeds to a figuring of the ethico-juridical context that does not reproduce the former. For the inhabitants of the cityscape, it requests a mode of participation that attends to an existence—both human and more than human—facilitated by colonial (total) violence. Now inhabitants of the city are always already a composite of different social (racial, gender-sexual, religious) collectives while at the same time deeply implicated in each and every other human and more-than-human composite that has, does, or might yet exist. Whether as citizens, permanent residents, or visitors, we thrive in cityscapes built on the extraction and expropriation of lands and the capacity to work of subaltern colonial subjects—that is, natives, slaves, and indentured laborers.

A matter neither of completion (of the modern project) nor of inclusion: no "proper" formulation of the question will render the left/radical/critical/ progressive political discourse finally complete. The racial question stands and awaits beyond the modern political text. For now, then, we might do with articulating the complications, contradictions, and complexities of an existence facilitated by extraction and expropriation. Perhaps what we need is not so much another version of the political discourse but a different kind of composition, a fragmentary and yet directed and intended one, that presents the racial question with all its difficulties and without apology.

Fig. 5
National Guard military members and African American men stand on a sidewalk during race riots, Chicago, 1919. Chicago History Museum (ICHi-065477).
Photo: Jun Fujita

Such a presentation of the racial question does not meet the criteria of the modern political discourse; actually it fails altogether. Ethically and aesthetically, however, such a composition might just get us a bit closer to the goal. For only such a composition—as a kind of text that articulates but does not resolve everything into a political position—might accommodate the ethical mandate to call into question our own existence. For there is a double demand to colonial residents, to all of us settlers: do not reproduce the violence and violations that have rendered our existence in occupied lands possible, *and* support (and, if invited, join in) the struggle for returning the land (and all the wealth derived from hundreds of years of extraction and expropriation) to its ancestral guardians. In Vancouver, where I am writing, they are the Squamish, Tsleil-Waututh, and Musqueam First Nations.

love of liberty and of democracy in consequence of the mass of the people, who in other countries might become mobs, being there nearly altogether composed of their own Negro slaves."

THE CONSEQUENCES OF 250 years of enslavement, of war upon black families and black people, were profound. Like homeownership today, slave ownership was aspirational, attracting not just those who owned slaves but those who wished to. Much as homeowners today might discuss the addition of a patio or the painting of a living room, slaveholders traded tips on the best methods for breeding workers, exacting labor, and doling out punishment. Just as a homeowner today might subscribe to a magazine like *This Old House*, slaveholders had journals such as *De Bow's Review*, which recommended the best practices for wringing profits from slaves. By the dawn of the Civil War, the enslavement of black America was thought to be so foundational to the country that those who sought to end it were branded heretics worthy of death. Imagine what would happen if a president today came out in favor of taking all American homes from their owners: the reaction might well be violent.

"This country was formed for the *white*, not for the black man," John Wilkes Booth wrote, before killing Abraham Lincoln. "And looking upon *African slavery* from the same standpoint held by those noble framers of our Constitution, I for one have ever considered *it* one of the greatest blessings (both for themselves and us) that God ever bestowed upon a favored nation."

In the aftermath of the Civil War, Radical Republicans attempted to reconstruct the country upon something resembling universal equality—but they were beaten back by a campaign of "Redemption," led by White Liners, Red Shirts, and Klansmen bent on upholding a society "formed for the *white*, not for the black man." A wave of terrorism roiled the South. In his massive history *Reconstruction*, Eric Foner recounts incidents of black people being attacked for not removing their hats; for refusing to hand over a whiskey flask; for disobeying church procedures; for "using insolent language"; for disputing labor contracts; for refusing to be "tied like a slave." Sometimes the attacks were intended simply to "thin out the niggers a little."

Terrorism carried the day. Federal troops withdrew from the South in 1877. The dream of Reconstruction died. For the next century, political violence was visited upon blacks wantonly, with special treatment meted out toward black people of ambition. Black schools and churches were burned to the ground. Black voters and the political candidates who attempted to rally them were intimidated, and some were murdered. At the end of World War I, black veterans returning to their homes were assaulted for daring to wear the American uniform. The demobilization of soldiers after the war, which put white and black veterans into competition for scarce jobs, produced the Red Summer of 1919: a succession of racist pogroms against

dozens of cities ranging from Longview, Texas, to Chicago to Washington, D.C. Organized white violence against blacks continued into the 1920s—in 1921 a white mob leveled Tulsa's "Black Wall Street," and in 1923 another one razed the black town of Rosewood, Florida—and virtually no one was punished.

The work of mobs was a rabid and violent rendition of prejudices that extended even into the upper reaches of American government. The New Deal is today remembered as a model for what progressive government should do—cast a broad social safety net that protects the poor and the afflicted while building the middle class. When progressives wish to express their disappointment with Barack Obama, they point to the accomplishments of Franklin Roosevelt. But these progressives rarely note that Roosevelt's New Deal, much like the democracy that produced it, rested on the foundation of Jim Crow.

"The Jim Crow South," writes Ira Katznelson, a history and political-science professor at Columbia, "was the one collaborator America's democracy could not do without." The marks of that collaboration are all over the New Deal. The omnibus programs passed under the Social Security Act in 1935 were crafted in such a way as to protect the southern way of life. Old-age insurance (Social Security proper) and unemployment insurance excluded farmworkers and domestics—jobs heavily occupied by blacks. When President Roosevelt signed Social Security into law in 1935, 65 percent of African Americans nationally and between 70 and 80 percent in the South were ineligible. The NAACP protested, calling the new American safety net "a sieve with holes just big enough for the majority of Negroes to fall through."

The oft-celebrated G.I. Bill similarly failed black Americans, by mirroring the broader country's insistence on a racist housing policy. Though ostensibly color-blind, Title III of the bill, which aimed to give veterans access to low-interest home loans, left black veterans to tangle with white officials at their local Veterans Administration as well as with the same banks that had, for years, refused to grant mortgages to blacks. The historian Kathleen J. Frydl observes in her 2009 book, *The GI Bill*, that so many blacks were disqualified from receiving Title III benefits "that it is more accurate simply to say that blacks could not use this particular title."

In Cold War America, homeownership was seen as a means of instilling patriotism, and as a civilizing and anti-radical force. "No man who owns his own house and lot can be a Communist," claimed William Levitt, who pioneered the modern suburb with the development of the various Levittowns, his famous planned communities. "He has too much to do."

But the Levittowns were, with Levitt's willing acquiescence, segregated throughout their early years. Daisy and Bill Myers, the first black family to move into Levittown, Pennsylvania, were greeted with protests and a burning cross. A neighbor who opposed the family said that Bill Myers was "probably a nice guy, but every time I look at him I see $2,000 drop off the value of my house."

WHITE FLIGHT WAS NOT AN ACCIDENT— IT WAS A TRIUMPH OF RACIST SOCIAL ENGINEERING.

Excerpt from Ta-Nehisi Coates, "The Case for Reparations," *The Atlantic* 313, no. 5 (June 2014): 64–65

30

The neighbor had good reason to be afraid. Bill and Daisy Myers were from the other side of John C. Calhoun's dual society. If they moved next door, housing policy almost guaranteed that their neighbors' property values would decline.

Whereas shortly before the New Deal, a typical mortgage required a large down payment and full repayment within about 10 years, the creation of the Home Owners' Loan Corporation in 1933 and then the Federal Housing Administration the following year allowed banks to offer loans requiring no more than 10 percent down, amortized over 20 to 30 years. "Without federal intervention in the housing market, massive suburbanization would have been impossible," writes Thomas

In the spring of 1921, a white mob leveled "Black Wall Street" in Tulsa, Oklahoma. Here, wounded prisoners ride in an Army truck during the martial law imposed by the Oklahoma governor in response to the race riot.

J. Sugrue, a historian at the University of Pennsylvania. "In 1930, only 30 percent of Americans owned their own homes; by 1960, more than 60 percent were home owners. Home ownership became an emblem of American citizenship."

That emblem was not to be awarded to blacks. The American real-estate industry believed segregation to be a moral principle. As late as 1950, the National Association of Real Estate Boards' code of ethics warned that "a Realtor should never be instrumental in introducing into a neighborhood ... any race or nationality, or any individuals whose presence will clearly be detrimental to property values." A 1943 brochure specified that such potential undesirables might include madams, bootleggers, gangsters—and "a colored man of means who was giving his children a college education and thought they were entitled to live among whites."

The federal government concurred. It was the Home Owners' Loan Corporation, not a private trade association, that pioneered the practice of redlining, selectively granting loans and insisting that any property it insured be covered by a restrictive covenant—a clause in the deed forbidding the sale of the property to anyone other than whites. Millions of dollars flowed from tax coffers into segregated white neighborhoods.

"For perhaps the first time, the federal government embraced the discriminatory attitudes of the marketplace," the historian Kenneth T. Jackson wrote in his 1985 book, *Crabgrass Frontier*, a history of suburbanization. "Previously, prejudices were personalized and individualized; FHA exhorted

segregation and enshrined it as public policy. Whole areas of cities were declared ineligible for loan guarantees." Redlining was not officially outlawed until 1968, by the Fair Housing Act. By then the damage was done—and reports of redlining by banks have continued.

The federal government is premised on equal fealty from all its citizens, who in return are to receive equal treatment. But as late as the mid-20th century, this bargain was not granted to black people, who repeatedly paid a higher price for citizenship and received less in return. Plunder had been the essential feature of slavery, of the society described by Calhoun. But practically a full century after the end of the Civil War and the abolition of slavery, the plunder—quiet, systemic, submerged—continued even amidst the aims and achievements of New Deal liberals.

TODAY CHICAGO IS one of the most segregated cities in the country, a fact that reflects assiduous planning. In the effort to uphold white supremacy at every level down to the neighborhood, Chicago—a city founded by the black fur trader Jean Baptiste Point du Sable—has long been a pioneer. The efforts began in earnest in 1917, when the Chicago Real Estate Board, horrified by the influx of southern blacks, lobbied to zone the entire city by race. But after the Supreme Court ruled against explicit racial zoning that year, the city was forced to pursue its agenda by more-discreet means.

Like the Home Owners' Loan Corporation, the Federal Housing Administration initially insisted on restrictive covenants, which helped bar blacks and other ethnic undesirables from receiving federally backed home loans. By the 1940s, Chicago led the nation in the use of these restrictive covenants, and about half of all residential neighborhoods in the city were effectively off-limits to blacks.

It is common today to become misty-eyed about the old black ghetto, where doctors and lawyers lived next door to meatpackers and steelworkers, who themselves lived next door to prostitutes and the unemployed. This segregationist nostalgia ignores the actual conditions endured by the people living there—vermin and arson, for instance—and ignores the fact that the old ghetto was premised on denying black people privileges enjoyed by white Americans.

In 1948, when the Supreme Court ruled that restrictive covenants, while permissible, were not enforceable by judicial action, Chicago had other weapons at the ready. The Illinois state legislature had already given Chicago's city council the right to approve—and thus to veto—any public housing in the city's wards. This came in handy in 1949, when a new federal housing act sent millions of tax dollars into Chicago and other cities around the country. Beginning in 1950, site selection for public housing proceeded entirely on the grounds of segregation. By the 1960s, the city had created with its vast housing projects what the historian Arnold R. Hirsch calls a "second ghetto," one larger than the old Black Belt but just as impermeable. More than 98 percent of all the family public-housing units built in

ARCHITECTURES OF CITIZENSHIP: SÃO PAULO OCCUPATIONS

PAULO TAVARES AND CARMEN SILVA

Nearly seven million families in Brazil live without adequate housing, yet it is estimated that the country has more than six million vacant urban properties. Hypothetically the housing deficit could be solved without building a single unit if empty buildings were converted into social housing. Since the 1990s various housing movements have claimed rights to the city by occupying vacant properties in downtown São Paulo. In September 2018 the curatorial team went to São Paulo to learn about the Movimento Sem Teto do Centro (City Center Homeless People's Movement), or MSTC, and its work with Ocupação 9 de Julho (July 9 Occupation), one of the strongest occupation movements in the city. In this conversation Carmen Silva, an MSTC leader, outlines her views on housing, architecture, citizenship, refugeeness, and politics in Brazil.

PAULO TAVARES: What is MSTC?

CARMEN SILVA: MSTC is a social movement that was created in response to the need for effective public policies in housing. But MSTC considers that housing doesn't mean only physical, fixed property. It has to be seen as a right, a basic right that stands for a number of other rights, such as health, education, culture, access. Today MSTC has a very explicit position: we don't want simply to create tenants; we want to create activists who have the understanding that they're citizens.

PT   It's not just the housing issue. The definition of housing that you are proposing is broader and more complex, involving all the elements that make a city.

CS   Much more complex: the house is the place where people have their moment of accommodation, but housing is much more than that. It is complete only when there are other sectors where people can act and exercise fundamental rights.

PT   I'd like to know a little about your story, Carmen. How did you get to São Paulo and become involved with the housing movement?

CS   I was born in Santo Estevão, in the Bahian Recôncavo
        region. I'm the daughter of a military man and a maid.
This is the Bahian context, isn't it? I was raised in lower-
middle-class social settings, but I studied at good schools.
I always had an uneasiness, a search for the freedom to
express myself as I wanted, to not follow the parameters of
the traditional family. In Bahia women are expected to get
married, to have children. Women study to some extent
but not to pursue a profession.

        At the time of the military dictatorship, there were many
social organizations, so there was that uneasiness of wanting
to speak more freely about Brazil, and I felt very repressed.
I worked in an urban transportation company in Salvador,
and I started attending union meetings. I suffered domestic
violence, and in the 1990s I decided to come to São Paulo.

        This is the exodus that we practiced: "I'll go to São Paulo,
which is one of the largest metropolises. On arriving there,
I will get a job, a house." It is a process of interterritorial refuge. And when I arrived here, I came across another Brazil.
It was a big disappointment. Then I found myself living in the
streets and went to a homeless shelter.

        At that time there were many *mutirões* [self-built
housing movements], which were on the periphery of the
periphery. At the shelter I met a woman who participated in
these community efforts, and she invited me to the meetings. The presence of Catholic pastoral care, which had a
sense of civic and political formation, was also very strong.
So I started attending the São José do Brás church, there
on Celso Garcia Avenue.

        At the church there was a housing group, and the
woman I met at the shelter took me there. At that moment
I began to understand São Paulo, because I began to
participate in its geopolitics. I began attending public hear-
ings, conferences, seminars, and I understood how the
state worked.

        I have eight children, and my story is the story of all
women who get divorced, all women who suffer domestic
violence and who continue to fight on their own. This memory is important for today's narrative, as this still happens
a lot. In the housing movement there are many women who
are heads of the family, who have gotten divorced and raised
their children by themselves and haven't had the opportunity to study. I have had the opportunity to study, and I
got involved in the movement out of a desire for freedom,
a desire to avoid being caught in that system.

PT   How was your experience living in the streets?

CS   It wasn't easy. There were several offers, offers that
        weren't good: prostitution and even crime. But I had a
clear goal, and if I didn't, I would be in a very complicated

situation today. At that time I got to know São Paulo better and met other people who were also living in the streets, so I began to better understand the struggle for housing. I wouldn't have this narrative that I have, to speak of the condition of the people who live in the streets, if I hadn't been through it myself. It was an experience that allowed me to grow and empower myself.

PT   Did MSTC already exist at that time?

CS   Not yet. Around 1995, 1996, besides the *mutirões* in the periphery, there were also tenement movements downtown. I got involved with those groups, and then we started a discussion with architects and other social movements about why we, as workers, had to live in the peripheral part of the city. Workers spend three, four hours a day inside buses. They often have to take two, three buses to get home, and their bosses don't pay the fare. So we began to discuss occupying downtown because it was totally empty at that time, with many vacant buildings. The financial center had moved to Avenida Paulista, and when that occurred, the center of the city was abandoned.

In November 1997 we occupied this building, Ocupação 9 de Julho, which was my second occupation. It was not MSTC yet; we occupied it as the Forum of the Tenements. In 1998 we occupied the old Matarazzo hospital, and afterward we occupied the Abolição, which was demolished. In 2000 we occupied the old Vila Formosa hospital, and then I and several other women—Ivanete de Araújo, Elizângela, Jaira, and others—created MSTC.

PT   MSTC and the downtown occupations in general are movements in which women have a very strong role in leadership. Why do you think the movement is shaped like that?

CS   First, by necessity: the lack of resources hits women first, as mothers and heads of the family. The woman is the first victim: she is homeless, she doesn't eat, she has to save money. The woman is by nature welcoming, she goes to the fight, she doesn't let herself be beaten so easily. We lead the confrontation, but at the same time we listen; we have the sensitivity to understand who the people with us are.

PT   You said something that I think is very important from the urban point of view. Initially the question of the struggle for housing was concentrated on the periphery, and then the movement turned to the center. This happened at a time when there were several "revitalization" initiatives in central São Paulo. Tell us a bit about this shift in perspective from the movement in relation to that "revitalization" process.

CS   In 1990, when we began to occupy the buildings, we
        were repopulating the central region. In the 2000s the
question of revitalization arose, and obviously the center
once again became the focus of capital speculation. Revital-
izing was a way of removing those who were already there.
These operations of revitalization lead to gentrification;
they don't seek a way for everyone to remain there. It is a
movement for certain people to be excluded.

PT   Housing isn't only about the ownership of a house; it has
        to do with the right to the city as a whole. Why occupy
the center of the city?

CS   First, because the central region is fully urbanized.
        There are public health resources, transportation,
mobility, culture, parks. In short, it has all the infrastructure
that supports human life. A house is simply a refuge, a place
where I can find peace and quiet to reinvigorate myself, but
housing must be seen as the whole context for life.

PT   In that sense you are offering an urban solution for
        improving the city as a whole, because the city becomes
more compact, more economical and sustainable, more
diverse.

CS   That touches on the environmental issue, for example.
        When you put three thousand families on a large plot of
land in a peripheral neighborhood, you are generating a huge
environmental and social problem. Without the minimum
urban infrastructure, terrible situations—such as floods,
precarious neighborhoods, and high levels of violence—
are created. They are actually ways of exiling people. There
are three thousand families, about six thousand people—
including children, young people, adults, and the elderly—
who don't have transportation, who don't have access to
health care, who don't have access to culture, who don't have
access to the city.

PT   How many occupations are there in the central region
        of São Paulo nowadays?

CS   In this region there are more or less fifty-one occu-
        pations recognized by city hall. But there are many
more, I believe, more than two hundred.

PT   São Paulo is an occupied city.

CS   It's an occupied city. And also by occupations that
claim to be legal. The Playcenter amusement park was occupying a public area. Several elite clubs in São Paulo are in
public areas.

PT   For capital the occupation is legitimized, while there is
      a whole condemnation of the popular classes, a process
of criminalization. How do you get organized to occupy a
building and turn it into popular housing?

CS   When we make the decision to make an occupation, it's
      always out of necessity but also to expose the lack of
effective housing policies. Several families from our foundational groups are being evicted and need a place to live.
But it is also important to show that the state is silent about
its obligations.

PT   The occupation is a way of making visible that these
      families are being forgotten and marginalized. It's a con-
crete form of exercising rights.

CS   You can't sit around waiting for your rights to come to
      you. Often you have to tell the state that you are aware
of your rights, and that requires action. Rights without
action are worthless.

PT   Collective action, isn't it? Tell us a little about how the
      occupations are organized.

CS   From the moment we go to occupy a building, there is
      already a collective organization. When you enter
a building, it is totally abandoned. The first thing we do is
organize a communal kitchen and also a maintenance team to
do the general cleaning, take out the garbage, and so on.
The movement does all the electrical work and painting, and
then we divide the spaces. Larger families get the biggest
spaces and so on. In this process mediators arise to help.
Rotating commissions allow all the residents to get involved
because everyone should have the opportunity to contrib-
ute. We delegate roles, and people are empowered. That's
very important.

PT   Earlier you referred to this collective dimension of the
      occupation as a "citizenship factory."

CS   When people join a movement, they all have their own
      problems. Here we try to show that other people's
problems aren't different from yours and that if we join
together, it gets much easier. If we are concerned only about
our own problems, nothing will be solved. We also offer help
on more concrete questions such as getting documents. We
provide information that they can't easily find out there; the
government doesn't offer it. So the movement really is a citizenship factory.

PT   Could we say that occupying is also a process of taking
      one's rights?

CS Yes, rights but also duties. The duty to respect one another, the duty to respect women, the elderly, children. It also has to do with participation. If you come to a meeting of the movement, you should go home and explain to your husband, or the two of you should come together and then explain to your children. Through all that, we are informing people, creating an understanding that our problem here, which is that of housing, is actually much broader.

PT A very recent phenomenon in the occupations of São Paulo is the arrival of refugees and migrants from other countries. Today, the occupations are inhabited by Bolivians, Palestinians, Syrians ...

CS Haitians, Congolese, Angolans, and others. In the 1970s, 1980s, 1990s, Brazil had a very serious problem, which was the internal exodus. The northeasterners came en masse to the great metropolis. Today, there are large displacements throughout the world, and Brazil has received these people. They come here and live in the streets. People arrive with a UN visa, which is temporary, and there is no planning for their entry. And where will they end up? In the occupations. Sometimes it is difficult to deal with; there is culture shock. But in the occupations there is no ghetto: there is a movement, there are people, there is humanity. And they also have to understand that this is a movement and not a government.

PT It's very interesting that occupations have become shelters for refugees. In Europe and elsewhere the official solution is refugee camps. But here in the occupations, they find a house, a place to dwell. It's a meaningful difference.

CS It's a big difference. I don't want anyone calling people foreigners, by the way. And they also have to participate in the movement, be part of the joint effort, the meetings.

PT There is a very strong relationship between MSTC and cultural movements. Ocupação 9 de Julho has become a cultural center in São Paulo. Here there are meetings, discussions. Now you've opened an exhibition space. Could you talk a little about the role of the alliances with artists, architects, and collectives that you have established over the years?

CS This network approach to other sectors is fundamental. Occupations should open their doors to the city. Culture is everything, so much so that it is the first thing this government wants to hit. Art is the only thing that carries everyone's voice to every sector.

PT   Tell me a bit about the role of architecture in the occupation.

CS   When we occupy a building, one of the first things we do is call the architects to accompany us on the first inspections. I know that every slab in this building can support five hundred kilos, between furniture and people walking around. I also know where I can get in with the heavy stuff and how I'll do the sewers, the electrical work. This is something the government should make available. The government comes only to accuse: "Built in an improper place. It's falling apart. It's causing floods. This work is irregular." There should be a body of architects in the city halls; the state should provide technical assistance.

PT   To conclude, I would like to talk about the situation Brazil is currently going through. What do you think of the future of housing movements in this context?

CS   For us nothing has ever been easy. There has always been a lot of fighting, a lot of persistence and struggle. And when you have a 1 percent caste that dominates Brazil, what happens? We will obviously be criminalized because where there is a social movement, there is organization and a collective context. And for the government, this isn't good, because the people who think collectively won't be deceived. When we occupy a place, it shows that you can maintain a community of people living well and with no need for government.

This conversation was recorded in São Paulo on April 1, 2019.

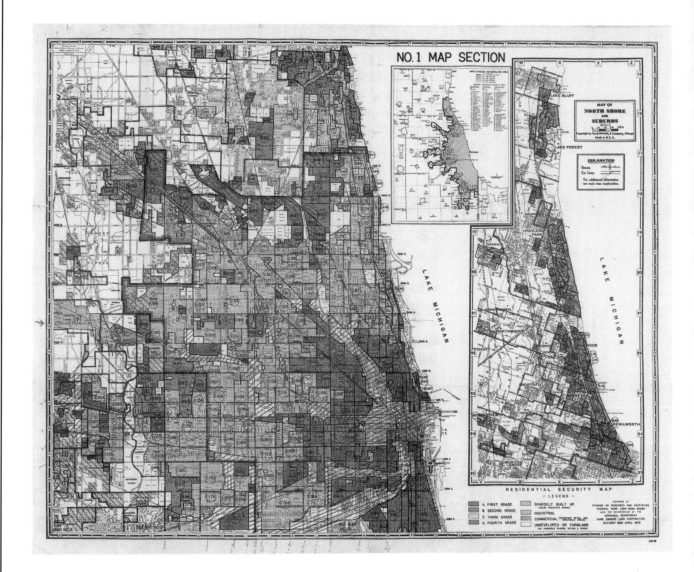

Chicago Residential Security Maps produced by the Home Owners' Loan Corporation, ca. 1930–40. National Archives, College Park, MD

In the United States the term *redlining* originally referred to the practice in the early twentieth century of systematically steering racial minorities into specific neighborhoods. It has since come to refer to the continued denial of resources and services to these neighborhoods' residents. The residential maps most often associated with the practice of redlining, however, contain no red at all. Instead the maps produced by the Home Owners' Loan Corporation (HOLC) between 1930 and 1940 rank residential values using lush pastels: a grassy green denotes so-called first-grade properties associated largely with stable white neighborhoods; sky blue and canary yellow, respectively,

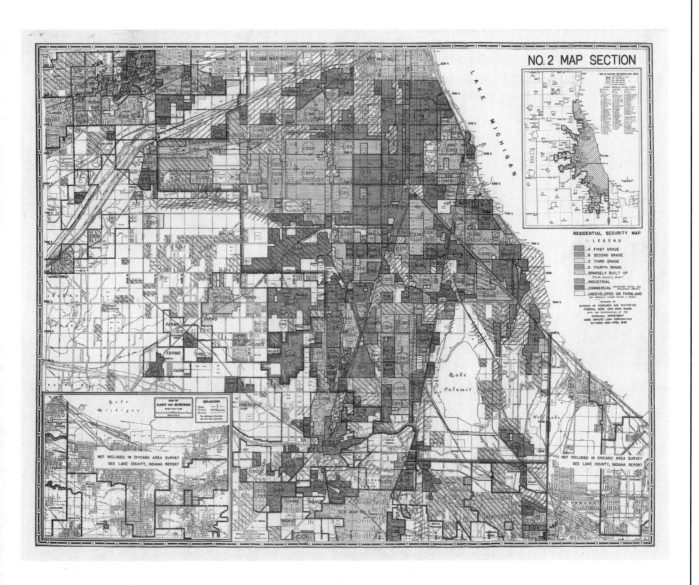

indicate second- and third-grade regions; and the lowest-rated, or fourth-grade, areas appear in a rosy pink. The HOLC made its maps in secret, intending these documents to circulate to a few select bureaucrats. Critics today disagree about how much the HOLC weighted race in its lending decisions, but its maps undoubtedly paved the way for more blatantly racist mapping procedures and policies carried out by both public and private lending agencies in the ensuing years. No one knows exactly how the HOLC used these maps. Their vibrant coloring suggests, however, that someone worked to make the maps appear visually pleasing even as they delivered damning assessments about neighborhoods. Inaugurating nearly a century of discriminatory residential practices, the HOLC maps do so in a color palette that buoyantly blunts their calamitous impact.
—Adrienne Brown

Protesters in front of a Chicago real estate office, 1966. Photo: Bernard Kleina

Martin Luther King Jr. is usually associated with civil rights campaigns in southern cities like Birmingham, Selma, and Montgomery, all in Alabama. But in 1966 King moved to Chicago for six months to participate in the Chicago Freedom Movement. Centered on open housing, the Chicago Freedom Movement targeted discriminatory practices in public housing, the rental market, and private ownership as essential to securing civil rights for blacks in the North. King acknowledged the challenges of fighting segregation in the American North. Whereas "in the South, we always had segregationists to help make issues clear," King observed, the "ghetto Negro has been invisible so long."

This photograph captures one of the movement's efforts to make the magnitude of northern housing segregation visible: organizing demonstrations against realtors who enforced the city's dual-market housing system. Protesters carry signs bearing the movement logo, which nests the letters MOVE into one symbol, denoting their efforts to "move slums together." It is likely that the mayor's office deliberately deployed black cops to the scene for the preferable optics. But the photograph also points to the thin line separating the officers—who wield batons resembling the sticks that support the protesters' signs and who were just as likely as those they surrounded to be discriminated against by Chicago realtors—from the activists.
—Adrienne Brown

CHICAGO FREEDOM MOVEMENT
DEMANDS FOR CREATING AN OPEN CITY

The following demands represent most of the conditions which create a system of domestic colonialism in which millions of Negroes are hopelessly trapped.

It is anticipated that community organizations will want to expand and elaborate on these demands in order that they may be presented to the City, State and Federal governments by Dr. Martin Luther King Jr. on June 26.

All community organizations are encouraged to submit demands necessary for changing conditions in their community by June 17.

I. EMPLOYMENT - INCOME - FINANCE

    A. CITY

        1. A public headcount by race in all city agencies;

        2. Fair employment in all city departments and administrative posts with special attention to fair employment in the higher paying jobs;

        3. A public statement of the headcount by race in all agencies from which the city purchases anything and from sub-contractors of these agencies;

        4. Fair employment in all companies and services providing goods and services for city departments;

        5. Mass transit facilities expanded to O'Hare and the northwest side to provide access for jobs and housing in northwest area from the south and west sides;

        6. Remove city and county funds from banks which discriminate in mortgage loans to Negroes.

(Continued)

B. STATE

    1. Enabling legislation to permit Chicago to levy an income tax;

C. FEDERAL

    1. A guaranteed annual income for all persons;

    2. A federal special economic development program for inner cities (like those in underdeveloped countries.);

    3. Minimum wage of $2.00;

II. HOUSING

A. CITY

    1. An open occupancy law;

    2. A program of 10,000 low-rent public housing units per year, integrated low and medium density units on scattered sites;

    3. A low interest direct loan program for rehabilitation and code compliance in owner-occupied structures-- with real estate tax abatement to the property and its improvements;

    4. An independent and revitalized Chicago Dwelling Association, providing middle-income housing proportionate to the need;

    5. Adopt New York City's program for emergency repair by the city with rents collected by the city to pay for repairs;

    6. Immediate improvement of all high-rise public housing projects--additional elevators, child-care centers on every third floor, locked lobbies, community facilities, protection, etc., and internal administrative changes;

    7. City services allocated according to population;

    8. A planned program of integration of all public housing/projects;

    9. Appointment of civil rights' representatives to all public bodies concerned with housing and planning;

(Continued)

ALMA DE BRONZE
(BRONZE SOUL)

VIRGINIA
DE MEDEIROS

...ing. I'm not alone and that's important. • In the MSTC movement, I found organization. Here I found strength and direction. H...

...ses: gastronomy, social insertion, English, carpentry, pre-college prep, theater, drawing, arts, cinema, capoeira, personal defen...

...n feed my son well and I couldn't do that before. Today I can provide leisure to my son and I couldn't do so before. This is an opp...

...ly. The genocide of the black population. The genocide took a lot of dear people to me, that struck me deeply. I, as a black wo...

..."Are you ready? It's a real fight! There'll be lots of fighting! Really lots of fighting!" I thought, "What will this fight be like?" Then...

...dignity. • We can be collective in everything in life. It's possible! We can share not only our shoulders but our space and our stor...

...more. My family cannot imagine how much I've changed, how much I've grown. And every day I learn, and every single day I ch...

...I did the orixás, a girl saw them and brought a friend from Switzerland to see them. The woman from Switzerland bought all th...

...udiced against. The MSTC movement leads you to the deconstruction of prejudice and rebuilds you for a libertarian movement...

...ather is 82 years old. Now he's got his own house. And even though he's got his home, he's still fighting. • Many politicians took...

...y took the life of a cousin of mine, she was blind. And they've also taken the life of my uncle. • I just can only thank the MSTC m...

...who loves cares for their loved ones. A good mother reprimands their child when it's necessary. That's love! That's taking care...

...er life. I crossed the border on foot because the money I had was just to buy a ticket. I consider myself a warrior. I used to be w...

...yone knows one another here. You can knock on your neighbor's door and ask for some rice, sugar and everyone shares it. Wh...

...hbor a sibling. • People have a biased look for the squats because they don't know what it's like living here. • Within the Housin...

...y years of domestic violence. I'm a survivor. Today I feel happy for being able to say to other MSTC women: It is possible, yes, t...

...ce station and ask for protective measures. • The municipal guard comes to visit MSTC women who are victims of domestic vic...

...ing harmony with all the powers that be. This is our daily struggle. • 80% of the members from the movement are single mother...

...neighbor, about social inclusion is our work tool. • We treat differences with dignity. Inclusion is key. • My son is 11 years old. H...

...nming. He always attends theater classes. If you have a gastronomy course, he has the certificate. He also took it. There is a g...

...I couldn't do that before. Today I can provide leisure to my son and I couldn't do so before. This is an opportunity available to o...

...auded me and said that the MSTC welcomes people who fight for their autonomy and studying is the way to that. I went to colle...

...tonomy that rises within us when we do what we like. That's something I learned within the MSTC. • When I lost my house, ju...

...ed here emotionally destroyed, soon I started breathing again and I was rebuilding myself. If your mind is quiet, you can think, ...

...ter. Here we receive people from several places with different ideas. This is the school of life. Here we learn what it is to live in ...

...never loses, it is because they're a fighting person who can be trusted. That reassured me. Carmen won a bid from the city an...

...g different, without acknowledging differences and without indifference. • Fighting for social rights that are not violated by the...

...al. • In the MSTC and in all of the housing movements are led by women who are on the front line. • At the Nove de Julho squat, ...

...e able to walk with my own legs. I want to be someone who matters in life. Within the MSTC movement, I am important! • Be...

...ana, practically inside a sewer. When it rained, everything flooded. One day, firefighters had to rescue me along with my chil...

...t right is that? We don't have that right. It's a lie. I've looked for it and it was nowhere to be found. But during the fight for the...

...ding on the 9 de Julho was amazing. I became someone else. It was my first squat. • When I moved to Sao Paulo, I came to work...

...it's my children who are going to study". I didn't have a chance. That's why I fight tooth and nail for my children to study. I say, ...

...r worker. But I say, it's still less, but we're going to change that reality. When I arrived in Sao Paulo, I didn't have any time off. N...

...op there. No. • All of us here at the MSTC movement are low-income workers. When we take part in squats, it is so that we can ...

...movement, I am another person. Today I feel like another woman. I feel strengthened. I have knowledge of my rights and my ...

...icipate in all of the acts because I reinforce my empowerment as a citizen and my conscience as a human being. • This feeling...

...eir condition or of their strength. • I'm in the right place. I'm in the right fight. That's what I want. Let's fight! Who doesn't figh...

...difficult. Living downtown changes everything. We have access and we have free time because we don't spend so much time...

...C movement. After that, she let my middle sister come live with me. Because where they live is difficult to study. Samanta came...

...movement includes culture in their fight. • When I lived on the outskirts, it took 3 hours inside public transportation to get to t...

...ge at 11:00 PM, picked up the last bus and arrived home at 1:00 AM. My mother would pick me up. I was worried she would pick m...

...always been based on care. I'm a fighter, like her. • vWhen I was 13 years old, my mother - so she could be able to pay the rent, sup...

...couldn't even leave, because the bosses wouldn't allow her to. There's still slavery in Brazil. The bosses think that you are their pr...

...calling us, saying, "My daughter, I can't go home because the bosses had an unforeseen situation." They never thought about he...

...her 3-year-old sister. I was the one who took care of the girls, took them to school, gave them lunch, bathed them, and studied...

...When I was able to pay our rent, my mother could save some money in the bank to buy our house. I was so happy! • I learned to...

...e is a very wonderful thing! • I, a black woman, resist. I resist. I, a black woman from squats, resist, and I will continue resistin...

...tancy. This is a place where one acquires political formation, social formation, and empowerment. • Here we have several cour...

...y benefits. All this comes from the Housing Movement. Housing comes with health, education, leisure, and culture! • Today I ...

...lable to all of MSTC's fighting companions. • I never felt like leaving Bahia, but there were many losses. Losses that struck me ...

...been a victim of domestic violence. The escape from genocide and femicide have brought me to Sao Paulo. • People used to say, ...

...it was a struggle for space, a struggle for one's own freedom, a struggle for one's own social credibility, a struggle for one's ov...

...es here intertwine in an unimaginable plot. Once you join the MSTC movement, you'll never be the same again. I'm not the sar...

...e and more. • There was an event here at the squat, Mrs. Carmen said that anyone who knew how to do the crafts could put the...

...s, about 20 pieces. I currently have an exhibition there. • The media distorts the meaning of the Housing Movement. I've alrea...

...as born and grew up amongst fights. My fight began as a child, my father fought for the homeless rural workers of Mato Grosso...

...ife of my family who fought for rural development. I cannot speak their names because they are very powerful and influentia...

true militancy. This is a place where one acquires political formation, social formation, and empowerment. • Here we have se

are many benefits. All this comes from the Housing Movement. Housing comes with health, education, leisure, and culture! • To

available to all of MSTC's fighting companions. • I never felt like leaving Bahia, but there were many losses. Losses that struck

e also been a victim of domestic violence. The escape from genocide and femicide have brought me to Sao Paulo. • People use

ood that it was a struggle for space, a struggle for one's own freedom, a struggle for one's own social credibility, a struggle for c

tories here intertwine in an unimaginable plot. Once you join the MSTC movement, you'll never be the same again. I'm not the s

e and more. • There was an event here at the squat, Mrs. Carmen said that anyone who knew how to do the crafts could put ther

about 20 pieces. I currently have an exhibition there. • The media distorts the meaning of the Housing Movement. I've already b

orn and grew up amongst fights. My fight began as a child, my father fought for the homeless rural workers of Mato Grosso do

of my family who fought for rural development. I cannot speak their names because they are very powerful and influential pec

Mrs. Carmen is like Sao Paulo - if you walk the line, you can have it all. Mrs. Carmen gives us some reprimands, you know? But

rmen develops this role very well! • I left my husband and my two daughters in Paraguay. I arrived alone in Brazil to try to ha

came strong when I came to live in the MSTC squat. Today I know more about Brazilian laws than about the laws of my count

u need from me, I'm here too. Everyone here is a friend. This is family! We don't have the relatives here in Brazil, but I conside

ent, through the MSTC, I was able to reach several goals. After 50 years, today I'm 54, I can go to college and graduate. • I suff

way from the domestic violence cycle. • When we hear there's a woman from the movement falling victim to violence, we go to

see if they are being well-assisted. • We have sought to participate in the Conference on Public Policies for Women. We are alv

se their children on their own. • Within the squat, you are not the lone individual, you are the collective individual. • Thinking al

s in a good school today. He does athletics at the Olympic Center in Sao Paulo. He studies English at a school downtown. He

eenagers here in the squat site, he also takes part in it. All that comes from the Housing Movement. • Today I can feed my son

TC's fighting companions. • I told Carmen, the leader of the movement, that I would like to join a social work college program.

aduated last year, 2017. When I finished college, Carmen invited me to oversee the Ocupação 9 de Julho squat. • Being indepen

ldn't defend me. But I didn't lose in the end, I am a winner! I have gained wisdom. I found a new family in the MSTC movemer

ct, you can take action. When you're destroyed, you can't see the forest for the trees. • I entered a squat and today I live in a Cult

ve environment. • Mrs. Carmen is a leader who never loses the squats. When I heard that, I already calmed down. If they're a pe

e of her squats will become a residential building, permanent housing financed by Caixa Econômica Federal. • We are all toge

tion makes me a fighter. I fight for the right to permanent housing, the right to education, the right to health, the right to a dign

all the efforts: building, cleaning, sanitizing, painting. • My family can take me in, but today I live in a place I identify with. I v

uthor of your own story is priceless! That's what Carmen Silva Ferreira, leader of the MSTC movement, teaches us. • I lived in

ed to pay 1,300 for the rent of this sewer. • Politicians say that since you are born you have the right to life, housing, education,

movement, I understood that those rights had to be fought for. • The MSTC movement is very organized. The day we occupiec

d, but I always wanted to study. My boss said, "When my children grow up, if you're still with me, you're going to study. But not i

n your studies, because studying makes you a better person". • Unemployment insurance for domestic workers is lower than for

s, we have start and finish times. We will acquire more rights. Existing is not enough, there has to be a right to life. We're not g

eyes of the rulers and demand public policies that meet our needs. • After I joined the fight, that I found this collective, that I fc

nd I know where to look for them, where to question them. And I want more than that! • I think it's extremely important for m

werment that I have is the same as that of many women here. Women who had been left and forgotten and who had no aware

! This is our motto. • I had the experience of working on the Jardins neighborhood and living in the extreme Southern Zone. It

es on public transportation. • My mother came from Porto Alegre and got to know the squat. She understood why I am part of

study and is fulfilling her dream. She got a scholarship and is taking a photography course. This is all thanks to the MSTC movem

e. I slept 4 hours a day, for 3 years, to be able to study. I used to leave my house at 5:00 AM to arrive at my job at 8:00 AM and

nd she was worried that I would go home by myself. It was very difficult. But we always took good care of ourselves, our relation

and raise money to buy a house of her own - started working at a job where she would only come home every 15 days and someti

hat you belong to them, that you don't have your own life and have to be at their disposal full time. My mother suffered. I remer

children. They never thought, "Are her children well? Are they alive?" I was 13 years old, the oldest one. I had an 8-year-old sister

m. I still worked at a sewing workshop beside my house to help my mother buy the house. I wanted my mother to come back to

conflicts and learned the feelings of others; it was the Housing Movement that taught me that. Learning to listen to other peo

alone and that's important. • In the MSTC movement, I found organization. Here I found strength and direction. Here I found

ronomy, social insertion, English, carpentry, pre-college prep, theater, drawing, arts, cinema, capoeira, personal defense. There

my son well and I couldn't do that before. Today I can provide leisure to my son and I couldn't do so before. This is an opportu

he genocide of the black population. The genocide took a lot of dear people to me, that struck me deeply. I, as a black woman, h

u ready? It's a real fight! There'll be lots of fighting! Really lots of fighting!" I thought, "What will this fight be like?" Then I unders

ty. • We can be collective in everything in life. It's possible! We can share not only our shoulders but our space and our stories.

ore. My family cannot imagine how much I've changed, how much I've grown. And every day I learn, and every single day I cho

l. I did the orixás, a girl saw them and brought a friend from Switzerland to see them. The woman from Switzerland bought al

prejudiced against. The MSTC movement leads you to the deconstruction of prejudice and rebuilds you for a libertarian movem

My father is 82 years old. Now he's got his own house. And even though he's got his home, he's still fighting. • Many politicians

They took the life of a cousin of mine, she was blind. And they've also taken the life of my uncle. • I just can only thank the M

Text excerpts on pp. 52–53 are taken from a series of twelve thirteen-minute videos de Medeiros created with members of Movimento Sem Teto do Centro (MSTC, City Center Homeless People's Movement) called *Quem não luta tá morto* (2016–18). Translated from Portuguese by Cecília Resende Santos.

Graphic Designer: Fernanda Porto
Photographer: Marcos Cimardi

First Image:
Alma de Bronze, 2016–18 (still). Video, 33 min.

Final Image:
Ocupação 9 de Julho (Nove de Julho Avenue Occupation), São Paulo, 2018

CHAPTER 2

APPEARANCES AND ERASURES

61

S. R. Crown Hall, Illinois Institute of Technology, Chicago, 2018. Courtesy Harboe Architects

In July 2018, during a maintenance excavation on the west side of S. R. Crown Hall, home to the College of Architecture at the Illinois Institute of Technology (IIT), workers unearthed the tiled basement floor of the Mecca Flats. This iconic apartment building in the Bronzeville neighborhood on Chicago's South Side was a center of African American culture in the first half of the twentieth century. The Mecca Flats was demolished in 1952 after more than a decade of conflict with residents and housing advocates who opposed its destruction. Crown Hall, a minimalist structure designed by Mies van der Rohe, took its place four years later.

AFRICAN SPACE MAGICIANS

LESLEY LOKKO

Chicago and Johannesburg are separated by hemisphere and history. Both have long histories of migration and segregation, diaspora and displacement, protest and prosperity. With ten million and eight million inhabitants, respectively, within their greater metropolitan areas, they are simultaneously outward and inward looking, famous for—and scarred by—their architecture, which plays a role that is at once literal and conceptual. Chicago is sometimes referred to as the "city of big shoulders," a reference to the many skyscrapers that line the shores of Lake Michigan. Johannesburg's northern suburbs form the world's largest man-made forest, trees planted by European settlers wishing to remake the landscape in an image (real or imagined) of that which they had left behind. Windy City, City of Gold, Chi-town, e-Goli ... affectionate nicknames abound.

Each city, in its own way, desperate to project an image of itself that in some way corresponds to the aspirations of its citizens—at least those with material and cultural capital.

But the brash confidence required to transform a "place of wild garlic"[1] into a metropolis of ten million people and an isolated, dusty farm atop a gold reef into one of the fifty largest urban areas in the world is also a foil for other, more hidden narratives, including complex and often contradictory relationships with the past and a stubborn inability to reconcile the historical geographies of race and class. For one who (although not native to either) has lived and worked in both cities for a number of years, the 2019 Chicago Architecture Biennial affords an unmissable opportunity to reflect on the myriad ways in which space both marks and is marked by memory, particularly in the context of oppression, resistance, and liberation. This text draws together a number of threads from seemingly disparate sources: architecture, alchemy, memory, and magic. It is rooted in South Africa's recent history, yet it speaks to the difficult relationship between power and place that is both the impetus for and the consequence of every act of settlement.

UMQAMBI WESINO
The Zulu term for an architect, *umqambi wesino*, is a haunting and beautifully complex phrase, meaning alternatively and in no particular order "magician of space," "maker of a situation," or "maker of a sensation." I can think of few equivalents in any language that so aptly describe the

1.
The name Chicago is derived from a French rendering of *shikaakwa*, the Indigenous Miami-Illinois word for a species of wild onion, *Allium tricoccum*, more commonly known as ramps. Wikipedia, s.v. "Chicago," last modified April 19, 2019, 21:06, en.wikipedia.org/wiki/Chicago.

2.
György Dalos, *The Guest from the Future: Anna Akhmatova and Isaiah Berlin* (New York: Farrar, Straus & Giroux, 1998).

3.
Anna Akhmatova, *Poem without a Hero*, in *"Requiem" and "Poem without a Hero,"* trans. D. M. Thomas (London: Eleck, 1976), 33.

4.
Nadine Gordimer, "Relevance and Commitment," in *The Essential Gesture: Writings, Politics, and Places*, ed. Stephen Clingman (London: Cape, 1988), 143.

5.
Ibid., 142.

strange alchemy that is the hallmark of the architectural process, from the idea or concept that first takes hold in the mind's eye, to the drawing forth of the design at various scales and from different perspectives through various media, to the explorations of scaled prototypes that test the architect's ability to resolve the tension between the imaginary and the "real" before the built form emerges. The synthesis between desire, which is often ephemeral, and result, often alarmingly material, is always a challenge. *Umqambi wesino* neatly circumvents this dilemma by positing a relationship between space, situation, and sensation and by introducing a new figure, the magician/maker. It's important to note, however, that the term does not refer to magic in the contemporary sense of the English word, with its connotations of trickery and sorcery, but rather to an ability to change states or shapes, closer to the Greek word *magikē tekhnē*, already etymologically linked to *archi-tekht*. In South Africa—where fierce battles over language, custom, ritual, and memory are still being fought—a unique opportunity exists for architects, and architecture, to play a different role, using different tactics and tools to stitch together conflicting accounts, possibly even to resolve them. It's a tall order.

GUEST FROM THE FUTURE

In his study of the Russian poet Anna Akhmatova, György Dalos examines what the publishers describe as "the most extraordinary encounter in the history of 20th century literature," the meeting between the fifty-six-year-old poet and the thirty-six-year-old philosopher Isaiah Berlin in Leningrad in 1945.[2] The two sat down at nine in the evening and talked for twelve hours straight. Neither gave a detailed account of their conversation, but after he left, she wrote a stanza in her epic work *Poem without a Hero,* in which she described him as "a man not yet appeared … strayed from the future."[3] The reference was taken up in 1979 by the South African Nobel Prize–winning writer Nadine Gordimer, at a conference at the University of Cape Town titled "The State of Art in South Africa." At the close of her speech, she stated: "Any optimism is realistic only if we, black and white, can justify our presence talking here, by regarding ourselves as what Mannoni, in his study of the effects of colonialism, terms 'apprentices to freedom.' Only in that capacity may we perhaps look out for, coming over the Hex River Mountains or the Drakensberg, that guest from the future, the artist as the prophet of the resolution of divided cultures."[4] Gordimer spoke of artists in the widest-possible sense of the word, including photographers, writers, playwrights, and architects. Both Akhmatova and Gordimer refer, albeit obliquely, to the alchemical processes that all artists employ in order to translate their *materiel*—in the French sense of the word as "stuff" or "matter"—into form. The daily transformations of reality are the artist's work, nowhere more acutely than in places undergoing dramatic political and social change.

But herein lies a contradiction, particularly for architects. Gordimer extended Akhmatova's

Fig. 1
Aerial view of Chicago, 1990s. Photo: Carol M. Highsmith / Buyenlarge / Getty Images

Fig. 2
Aerial view of Johannesburg, 2013. Photo: Dean Hutton / Bloomberg via Getty Images

description of Berlin by drawing an analogy between freedom and the "future," putting forth a compelling vision of the artist/architect as a "prophet," someone—perhaps the only one—capable of reconciling a divided culture. The impetus to change, transform, remake the world is, according to Gordimer, innate: "It is in [the nature of artists] to want to transform the world, just as it is a political decision for those who are not artists."[5] Architecture may be viewed as the most overtly political of the "plastic" arts, at least in a corporeal sense. No other discipline has as immediate and permanent effect on the way we live and view the world. As Winston Churchill famously said, "We shape our buildings; thereafter they shape us." Individual buildings aside, cities cement our attitudes toward one another through a complex web of policy, capital, fear, and desire.

While it's true that cultures are divided in myriad ways, no division I can think of has proved more resistant to long-term equitable and inclusive resolution than *race*. What we mean when we use the term differs from society to society, culture to culture, of course. As with the word *culture*, there is no clear consensus on what *race* means, let alone what it actually is. Skin color? Heritage? Ancestry? Ethnicity? Irrespective of how we define it, the history of human settlement is predicated on the divisions we project onto those who are not "of our tribe." If, as Richard Sennett has argued so persuasively, the "city is the place where we encounter those who are not like us," our ongoing difficulties in reconciling our attitudes toward

Fig. 3
Noero Wolff Architects, Red Location Museum, Port Elizabeth, South Africa, 2006. Photo: Iwan Baan

Fig. 4
Cristina de Middel, *Hamba*, from the series *Afronauts*, 2011. Photo: Cristina de Middel / Magnum Photos

Fig. 5
Project review at the University of Johannesburg Graduate School of Architecture (GSA), 2017

"others" suggest that four thousand years of communal living have done little to heal the scars of our projections.[6]

THE HERITAGE INDUSTRY

Segregationist policies everywhere rely on a sense of order that is enforced through aggressive legal and policing frameworks, as well as the tacit consent of the majority of the population, until such time as the center cannot hold, to evoke Chinua Achebe.[7] Apartheid is perhaps the most extreme example of the power of the state to shape and control the lives of its citizens, but like all South African cities, including and especially Johannesburg, Chicago and other American cities still carry the scars of centuries of racial and economic inequity owing to slavery and segregationist policies. Systemic oppression survives on an outward show of strength, but as history has shown us time and again, no system—no matter how strong— remains in place forever. In many ways the heritage "industry"— which packages and contains the formal and culturally approved version of events through museums, archives, exhibitions, texts, and so on—struggles to find the appropriate form or means to tell "alternative" histories, particularly those that run counter to the official narratives.

Several years ago I visited Jo Noero's prizewinning Red Location Museum near Port Elizabeth, South Africa, which now stands dilapidated and permanently closed. Located in the neighborhood where the African National Congress was founded, it won several prestigious architectural

6.
Richard Sennett, *Together: The Rituals, Pleasures and Politics of Cooperation* (New Haven, CT: Yale University Press, 2012), iv.

7.
In the title of his novel *Things Fall Apart* (1958), Achebe evoked William Butler Yeats's poem "The Second Coming" (1919), specifically the line "Things fall apart; the centre cannot hold."

8.
Richard Sennett, *Building and Dwelling: Ethics for the City* (New York: Farrar, Straus & Giroux, 2018), 35. See also Martin Heidegger, "Building Dwelling Thinking," in *Basic Writings*, ed. David Farrell Krell (San Francisco: Harper Collins, 1992), 347–63. *Omnis aetas* is a Latin phrase meaning "critique of the work."

awards, but local residents have accused the city of "building a house for dead people" while they continue to live in squalor. At the time of my visit, undertaken with architecture students from the University of Cape Town, the museum was pristine, awaiting inauguration. I noticed that the signs were in three languages—English, Afrikaans, and Xhosa—and that the Xhosa translations of "standard" museum signage—Entrance, Exit, Shop, Restaurant, and so on—were sometimes four or five words long. Curious about the exact translations, I asked a security guard to explain why the phrase for "museum exit," for example, appeared to be a completely different phrase from "museum entrance." He was baffled by the question at first but then grasped what I was trying to ask: "What is the Xhosa word for museum?" He consulted with a colleague for a few minutes, then returned.

"Actually, we don't have a word for that."

"So what do you call a place like this?" I gesture to the building around me.

They exchange a quick glance. "This place," his colleague interrupts coldly, "is a place for white people."

"So what do you call the building where you go to remember something?" I ask after a moment.

They both look at me incredulously. "Madam, we don't need a building for that."

It remains one of the most powerful conversations I have ever had about architecture, anywhere.

Post-1994, museums "celebrating" the formal end of apartheid have sprung up like mushrooms in almost every municipality. Some are genuinely interesting, at least in terms of their architectural merit, others less so. For the most part they follow a tried-and-tested typology of museums and archives everywhere, due in part to public building codes, which cannot be easily ignored. The programmatic aspects dominate the form: entrances, exits, ramps, toilets, offices, exhibition spaces, and so on. One of the more puzzling conundrums, however, is the lack of experimentation in terms of what the appropriate container of history might be. As evidenced in the short conversation quoted above, we might begin to think differently about formal ideas associated with memory, history, past, present, and, critically, the future. The task for would-be African space magicians might be to rethink the spatial, formal, and material relationship between program and form or between landscape and building, inside and outside, memory and imagination, to name but a few of the binaries that dominate conventional architectural expressions of remembrance.

OMNIS AETAS
To paraphrase Richard Sennett, who, in turn draws on Heidegger, "people move through a space and dwell in a place."[8] One reading of a third place—the academy—is the space/place in which we learn how to do both. Schools of architecture have a long history of being either efficient training camps for industry or hotbeds of radical resistance and innovation. Sometimes—though admittedly rarely—a single school is both. The Graduate School of

9.
Report to the Graduate School of Architecture, University of Johannesburg, from the South African Council for the Architectural Profession (SACAP) Validation Visiting Board (April 16–18, 2019).

10.
Achille Mbembe, "Decolonizing Knowledge and the Question of the Archive," lecture delivered at Wits Institute for Social and Economic Research, University of Witwatersrand, Johannesburg, wiser.wits.ac.za/content/achille-mbembe-decolonizing-knowledge-and-question-archive-12054.

11.
For a more comprehensive reading of Transformative Pedagogies, see http://www.gsa.ac.za/news-events/latest-news/transformative-pedagogies/.

Architecture at the University of Johannesburg was set up in 2014 with the explicit intention to make and unmake the architectural canon against the backdrop of the student protests of the previous four years, which effectively shut down tertiary education. Interestingly, the protest that ignited demands around the world for a decolonized and transformed curriculum was itself directed against a memorial, a statue erected in honor of a man (Cecil Rhodes) whose legacy divides the country to this day.

Transformative Pedagogies was a teaching and research program that sought to transform both the way we teach architecture and what we teach. Adopting the renowned "unit system" teaching methodology pioneered by Alvin Boyarsky at the Architectural Association in London in the 1970s, it attempted to challenge the blended tripartite model of South African architectural education (British, Bauhaus, and Beaux-Arts) by insisting on creating a "safe" space for black students to fashion their own architectural narratives, often through highly speculative and experimental means. In many ways the initiative came at precisely the right moment. The political uncertainty that followed the protests created a pedagogical vacuum, which in turn made room for other curriculum changes, the most important of which was the shift from semester-long to yearlong programs. Having the "extra" time to develop and explore alternative methods and means of representation also allowed students to take on much more complex and challenging issues: from the history of the black diaspora, creolization, migration, language, and identity to contemporary challenges of informality, participatory practice, and politics. Yearlong studios also allowed students to work in a more genuinely interdisciplinary way, synthesizing knowledge from related disciplines such as literature, landscape architecture, sociology, and anthropology.

What began as an experiment with eleven students has now morphed into a school of almost one hundred postgraduate students, a tenfold increase. The Graduate School of Architecture is now Africa's largest dedicated postgraduate school of architecture, but its place and future are far from assured. Staffing remains its biggest challenge: although its early focus was undoubtedly on giving students the agency and space literally to remake the canon, one of the unforeseen results has been a sudden and dramatic upsurge in young teachers. Approximately 60 percent of the teaching staff have graduated in the past three years; many have formed collaborative offices and regard the school as an essential lifeline in sustaining livelihoods and interest in the debates. It has had an impact on the way students view the profession as a whole: less "professional" and vocational, perhaps, and more as a way of questioning wider societal issues.

It remains to be seen whether this is sustainable: built-environment professions are notoriously volatile. In the context of a weakening overall economy, the risks are magnified. The school's commitment to fashioning a culture of open-ended dialogue has been tested at several points over the past five years, most recently in the visit by the country's accrediting body, the South African Council for the Architectural Profession. After robust and difficult conversations, which centered on the perceived lack of professional and technical competencies within students' work, the council concluded, "The proportion of black students within the GSA is notable as amongst the highest of any Master's programme in South Africa. It is evident that one of the key successes of the application of the Unit System has been the creation of space for black students to find their voice and express their architectural identity through their research and design work, an important step against the backdrop of the agenda for the decolonisation of higher education."[9]

In a lecture given in 2015, the Cameroonian scholar Achille Mbembe brilliantly unpacked the terms *decolonization* and *transformation*:

> When we say *access*, we are also talking about the creation of those conditions that will allow black staff and students to say of the university: "This is my home. I am not an outsider here. I do not have to beg or to apologize to be here. I belong here."
>
> Such a right to belong, such a rightful sense of ownership has nothing to do with charity or hospitality.
>
> It has nothing to do with the liberal notion of "tolerance."
>
> It has nothing to do with me having to assimilate into a culture that is not mine as a precondition of my participating in the public life of the institution.
>
> It has all to do with ownership of a space that is a public, common good.
>
> It has to do with an expansive sense of citizenship itself indispensable for the project of democracy, which itself means nothing without a deep commitment to some idea of public-ness.[10]

Five years into the "experiment," I would argue that the question of what constitutes an authentic African architectural culture is premature. Protecting the space in which such a culture may develop and mature is the school's fundamental priority.[11]

Now the way of the Mecca was on this wise.

Excerpt from Gwendolyn Brooks, *In the Mecca: Poems* (New York: Harper & Row, 1968), 4, 5

Sit where the light corrupts your face.
Miës Van der Rohe retires from grace.
And the fair fables fall.

S. Smith is Mrs. Sallie. Mrs. Sallie
hies home to Mecca, hies to marvelous rest;
ascends the sick and influential stair.
The eye unrinsed, the mouth absurd
with the last sourings of the master's Feast.
She plans
to set severity apart,
to unclench the heavy folly of the fist.
Infirm booms
and suns that have not spoken die behind this
low-brown butterball. Our prudent partridge.
A fragmentary attar and armed coma.
A fugitive attar and a district hymn.

Sees old St. Julia Jones, who has had prayer,
and who is rising from amenable knees

5

Mecca Ten

Residents of the Mecca Flats meet to oppose the building's demolition, Chicago, 1950. Courtesy Chicago History Museum (ICHi025338)

The Mecca Flats had prestige—not because of the architecture, though it was remarkable, but because of the kind of people who lived in or near the building. In the first half of the twentieth century, residents included African American bankers, professionals, businessmen—such as Anthony Overton and Jesse Binga—and important musicians and artists. Together they invigorated the neighborhood and helped form the Stroll, the stretch of State Street that served as the culture and entertainment center of Bronzeville and the entire Black Belt (or the "ghetto," as others called it).

The Mecca Flats gave physical form to the history and positive aspects of the Black Belt. The successful people who lived there were role models for members of the African American community whose families had fled the South looking for a better way to live. That was true until

ts Fight — 1950

after World War II, when the population of the neighborhood began to change. The second wave of the Great Migration brought to Chicago a new influx of African Americans who were socially, culturally, and economically less fortunate than those who arrived in the first phase, from roughly 1916 to 1940.

It was also in that period that the Illinois Institute of Technology began building a new campus, designed by Ludwig Mies van der Rohe, to accommodate a growing student body. The institute was able to capture almost all the space surrounding its original campus and planned to raze the buildings in that area in a process of "urban renewal." The Mecca Flats was a victim of that process. For people who lived in the building and their relatives and friends, the building was emotionally and historically very precious. They wanted the building landmarked and saved from demolition, and so they protested, unsuccessfully.

—Timuel Black

73

A partly demolished tower at the Cabrini-Green public housing project, Chicago, 2006.
Photo: Paul D'Amato

The words "Cabrini-Green Homes" stir the imagination in Chicago and beyond. The curious Day-Glo colors of this partially demolished public housing project hint at the vibrant communities that once lived there. These residents formed complex support and friendship networks while facing myriad challenges: crumbling architecture due to deferred maintenance, police acting with impunity and brutality, and strategic disinvestment due to urban renewal policies that privileged some Chicago communities while negatively impacting others.

Erected between 1942 and 1961, this seventy-acre development located between Lincoln Park and the Gold Coast—two of Chicago's wealthiest neighborhoods—was initially regarded as a source of salvation for Chicago's poor. Over time, systemic forms of racism, including federally sponsored systems of segregation like redlining and the growth of the prison industrial complex, shifted the demographics of Cabrini-Green's residents from multiracial to predominantly African American. By the mid-1970s, Cabrini-Green, the setting of both the television sitcom *Good Times* and the Hollywood horror film *Candyman*, became synonymous with the problems of public housing and the many stereotypes about what it meant to be poor and black in the United States.

Yet Cabrini-Green was home to many communities Chicago had otherwise cast off. The battle to save the development from demolition in the mid-1990s is part of a larger narrative of the dismantling of community services and a diminishing commitment to public welfare in the United States. When 1230 North Burling Street, the last of Chicago's high-rise public housing projects, was demolished on November 16, 2015, the residents of Cabrini-Green were forced out to make room for white middle-class homeowners as part of America's mixed-income housing experiment.
—Lisa Yun Lee

DECOLONIZING SPACE: THE CASE OF #RHODESMUSTFALL

YESOMI UMOLU, INAM KULA, AND AVIWE MANDYANDA

In March 2015 students at the University of Cape Town began demonstrating to demand the removal of a statue of the British businessman and colonial-era politician Cecil John Rhodes. On his death in 1902 Rhodes bequeathed the land on which the university was built, but he was also responsible for the slaughter of thousands of Africans and helped to pave the way for apartheid. The statue was removed in April 2015, but the student protestors continued to pursue their broader goal of transforming educational institutions in South Africa. Here Inam Kula and Aviwe Mandyanda speak with Yesomi Umolu about their participation in student activism as South Africans born after the end of apartheid as well as the political and social implications of the design and use of public space.

YESOMI UMOLU: In 2015 a series of student-led protests were mobilized in South Africa around a campaign calling for the removal of a statue commemorating the British colonialist Cecil John Rhodes at the University of Cape Town [UCT]. How did these protests influence our understanding of how memory functions within public space in contemporary South Africa? Why was it important to call for the removal of this statue?

INAM KULA: The Rhodes Must Fall (#rhodesmustfall) movement was motivated by the fact that Rhodes was a colonialist who exploited black people but continued to stand tall in the middle of a university campus in Africa. The students participating in these protests were challenging the ways in which public spaces in South Africa continue to privilege white bodies over black bodies. Public spaces are the terrain of contestation of ideas and thus are never free from the risk of disorder. Rhodes Must Fall brought disorder to the fore, not for its own sake but rather as a means to express the centuries of violence against black people. The protests called for a process of decolonization, seeking to center black people in the discourse of architecture and space, and also for black people to be recognized as human beings and as a community with a history. For South Africans it is important that our surroundings not only invoke the memory of our brutal past but also reflect our desires and aspirations as a people.

AVIWE MANDYANDA: Rhodes Must Fall highlighted the fact that the statue was at odds with its context. And by context I mean public memory and history. The movement argued that the Rhodes statue was a form of selective memory. Its posture and symbolism served to erase and antagonize black people. Colonial statues still exist because, at the core, universities and the country at large remain untransformed. Rhodes contributed to the creation of the university through the exploitation and exclusion of black people and women; in fact, he was quoted as saying that he would build the university on the sweat and blood of black people. The feminist bloc within the movement argued that the statue represented a hypermasculinity that symbolized misogyny and patriarchy. In a postcolonial and culturally diverse society, how do we contend with a statue that celebrates a colonialist history?

YU   The protests centered on a call for decolonial practices that extended from public space into the space of institutions. This is particularly evident in the evolution of the Rhodes Must Fall movement into the Fees Must Fall movement, which sought to curtail the costs of higher education in South Africa and to highlight institutional racism within the education sector. Why did these two protest moments evolve at this particular moment in South African history?

IK   The only history that we're taught in schools is that of European culture. This is reflected in our curricula, anthems, buildings, and town names, for example. My generation grew up not knowing what it really means to be African, and when we are taught about our Africanness, it's usually as a footnote to European history or with reference to our presumed barbarism. This is a form of pedagogy that teaches black children to undermine if not hate their beings. The protests were an awakening that allowed us to articulate the challenges of studying and living in a society that erases and distorts our history. In my view it is only the "born-free" generation that could be so radical in asking these questions, because of our positionality and our lack of experience of apartheid.

AM I think the protests were almost bound to happen. According to James Baldwin, the paradox of education is that the more educated one gets, the more conscious one becomes of one's surroundings. A crucial factor in the protests was that they represented an increasingly diverse student body. It is this community that should then be represented in public monuments, and this community's history should also be presented truthfully. For this student community the Rhodes statue, along with the university's norms and traditions, simply did not represent the contributions of black people to South African history.

YU   An interesting facet of both these protest movements, like many such events worldwide, is that public space is often the locus of activism. In the case of Rhodes Must Fall, however, a public monument was not just a backdrop but was the entity that was being contested. Likewise, with Fees Must Fall, students were protesting the tangible and intangible infrastructure (architecture) of higher education. We know from the long history of apartheid in South Africa that architecture and public space became tools for white hegemony and black oppression. Can you speak to the relationship between architecture and power in the South African context, in both the past and the present?

IK   The landlessness of black people in the colonial and apartheid eras affected their identity, their culture, and their sense of being. Apartheid was founded on the systemic separation between blacks and whites, creating two separate communities. The black community was violently subjected to inhumane conditions and was restricted in terms of where people could live and work, whereas the white community had freedom of space and ownership. Michel Foucault argued that since the eighteenth century, with the increased discourse between architecture and space-making practices and political dialogue across the world, governments have used architecture to retain power. We can see these principles in the governance of South Africa during apartheid and in the making of our cities and public spaces.

AM   It is interesting that within the Rhodes Must Fall and Fees Must Fall movements, students occupied and reclaimed colonial architectural spaces as spaces of power. For example, at the University of the Witwatersrand, students used the Senate House building, one of the main administrative buildings on campus, to hold mass meetings, thereby reclaiming it as a space where students' voices could be heard. Another space of power was the street. The street was used strategically to protest within the city, bringing the social and economic conditions of education to the forefront of the national debate. It is striking how the student movement redefined spaces on campus and in the city through everyday practices of protest.

YU   It took the actions of someone who was not an architecture student, Chumani Maxwele, to instigate the Rhodes Must Fall movement, which in some way problematizes the role of the architect and planner. How do the study and practice of architecture contend with the colonial imaginary? How do the practices of architecture and planning struggle to confront and challenge the fraught relationship between space and power in the South African context?

IK   Yes, it took not architects, not urban designers, nor heritage practitioners, but a group of black students to initiate a robust conversation around the importance of considering race and of centering black people in architecture and its history. The primary reason for this is that architecture and its study have been comfortable with the erasure and subordination of the memory of black people. In my view the entire cohort of white scholars currently working in the discipline of architecture do not see anything wrong with maintaining the remembrance of a history that brutalizes black people and reduces them to objects in their own country of birth. This speaks to the lack of transformation in the field. This thinking directly affects the type of students that matriculate from architecture schools.

Personally, as a third-year student at the time of the protests, even though I had read so much literature on the relationship between space and power in the South African context, I couldn't use my education or tangible architectural and spatial interventions to express the problems within our university. I think this was a result of my own cognitive dissonance as a student who is black and has been marginalized for so long and is also studying under an educational system that prioritizes Western knowledge. I was not able to reconcile the two, and ultimately my humanness/being had to be compromised for a discipline that does not value my heritage. From the history and the theory to the design briefs we receive, nothing is inclusive or representative of African heritage and lived conditions. An example of this was one of my first-year history and theory of architecture assignments. Here a group of us were assigned to analyze and compare the Rhodes Memorial with the Thomas Jefferson Memorial. On commencing the research, I discovered that Rhodes was an imperialist responsible for the genocide of many Africans. The project brief was not concerned with this, however, but rather with the columns, the scale, and the symmetry of the monument.

AM I completely agree. For us it has been very difficult to challenge the status quo. The student protests gave us the platform and also the language to articulate what is wrong with the university. But it is through reading outside the curriculum that we have been able to articulate and address these issues.

For example, I am part of a collective of students and graduates called BlackStudio that formed within the School of Architecture and Planning at the University of the

Witwatersrand a couple of years prior to the student protests. Our work has focused on the relationship between blackness and space. Many of the methods of planning or making architecture appear alien when we go into black spaces such as the townships. So we work toward unpacking these spaces on their own terms, as spaces of possibility, as opposed to spaces of lack. We believe that there is more that these spaces can tell us about their own desires and their own futures than what we tend to impose on them. We adopt an understanding of space that is inspired by the thinking of black scholars and activists such as Frantz Fanon and Steve Biko in addition to radical black feminists such as Pumla Dineo Gqola, Oyeronke Oyewumi, and Audre Lorde. The reach of BlackStudio has gone beyond the university. We have held winter schools in townships and rural areas of South Africa. In 2016 we hosted an exhibition titled *Makoporosh—it takes a village to raise a child*, in which we built a 1:1 scale interactive township space approximately 120 square meters in size with the intention of exploring and understanding the nature of interaction, community, and social behaviors in black spaces. We also host BlackStudio Talks, inviting the public to debate and discuss black spatial explorations guided by both theory and lived experiences.

YU   How have you come to imagine a decolonial process within the field of architecture? How does one make decolonized spaces or architectures?

AM   For us at BlackStudio it is important for black architects and urbanists to occupy space and discourse. There is often no space for decoloniality to take place within institutions. The name BlackStudio therefore came about because we felt we were always in "white studio" at the Wits School of Architecture and Planning. By this we mean that we were being taught only white ways of understanding cities and architecture, by predominantly white lecturers. So we took a space in the center of the school's building and turned it into a BlackStudio space, where we worked collaboratively to make sense of what it means to be black in our disciplines and initiated various projects that engaged with understanding black urban space and architecture as well as experiments in possible African futures. We have also found that working with other disciplines in a collaborative manner should be at the foundation of any decolonial project.

IK   Our call for a free decolonial education has not yet materialized. As a first step we need to decommodify in order for our education to empower us to go out into society and make a difference. The discourse about the relationship that black people have with space should be spearheaded by those who have the lived experience of being black. We also need to look at architecture and space-making practices through a South African lens. We need to center South African issues and cities as a basis for trying to understand ourselves instead of engaging in a process of othering. When we start looking at cities, architecture, and space from an African vantage point, this allows for new insights that push the boundaries of established knowledge. There needs to be an alternative framework that speaks to our lived conditions and experience.

YU   The statue of Rhodes was eventually removed. Was this understood as a success? As we know, power articulates itself in tangible and intangible forms. Do we take the removal of the statue as a completion of the decolonial process? Or is there more to come?

IK   The reality is that Rhodes is not gone. He exists both tangibly and intangibly on our campus, in our city, and in our country. For example, there is still the Rhodes Memorial near the UCT campus, which people visit daily. But of course the call for Rhodes to fall was never about the statue alone; rather, it is about the structural violence that we as black students and black people as a whole face on our campuses and in our society at large. The dehumanizing conditions that result from land dispossession are not gone, even though black people achieved freedom in 1994. The hierarchies that existed during apartheid are still intact. We are in limbo in terms of the decolonial process at the moment.

AM   I agree. The movement represented much more than the removal of the statue. It was important to have a national debate around symbolism, memory, and decolonization in our public spaces. The movement made it clear that some histories have been erased while others have been upheld. Of course we must not take for granted the impact of the statue's removal. I remember seeing YouTube videos of the removal in which people were crying with excitement because public monuments not only connect us to the past but also affect how we feel in the present. Removal of these symbols of colonialism and patriarchy is very important in enabling us to recontextualize history. The removal of the statue was in fact a moment of making history. The process of decolonization is incomplete, however; it is an ongoing struggle.

This conversation was recorded via Skype between Chicago and Cape Town on April 28, 2019.

APPEARANCES AND (NON)ERASURES:

MAPPING CONFEDERATE MONUMENTS AND THE RADICAL CONDITIONEDNESS OF LIBERATION

MARIO GOODEN

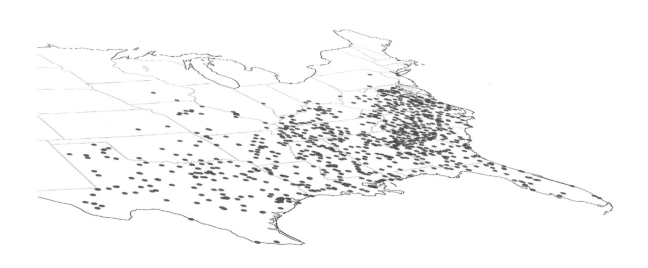

As of February 1, 2019, the Southern Poverty Law Center identified 1,747 Confederate monuments, place-names, and other symbols still in public spaces, both in the South and across the United States.

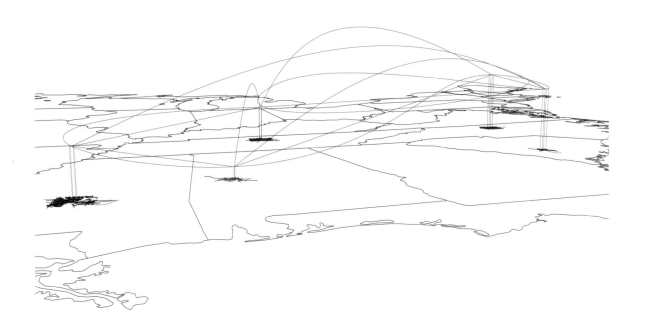

Confederate Soldiers Monument, Greensboro, North Carolina

TITLE: Confederate Soldiers Monument, Greensboro

ARTIST(S): Bakewell & Mullins, Salem, OH, Sculptor

DATE: September 26,1888

MEDIUM: NA

PHYSICAL LOCATION: Green Hill Cemetery, 901 Wharton St, Greensboro, NC

LONG DESCRIPTION:

1888 Inscription: OUR / CONFEDERATE DEAD / 1861-65 / DEDICATED TO THE / MEMORY OF / 300 UNKNOWN SOLDIERS / BY THE LADIES' / MEMORIAL ASSO. OF / GREENSBORO, N.C.

November 17, 2017 addition to inscription: WHICH BECAME / DAUGHTERS OF THE CONFEDERACY / GUILFORD CHAPTER 301, 1899

Base Inscription, top of upper base: ERECTED IN 1888

1969 Plaque, front of upper base: RESTORATION MAY 10, 1969 / ELIHU WALKER CAMP 1290 / SONS OF CONFEDERATE VETERANS

1984 Plaque, front of middle base section: 2ND RESTORATION MAY 10, 1984 / COL. JOHN SLOAN CAMP 1290 / SONS OF CONFEDERATE VETERANS

Description: The Confederate Monument at Green Hills Cemetery marks the mass grave of approximately 300 unknown Confederate soldiers. It features the statue of a soldier wearing a great coat and kepi (cap) with his proper left foot slightly in front of the right. The musket butt rests on the ground and is gripped by the proper right hand with the left arm resting on the end of the weapon's barrel. The statue was formed of stamped copper and manufactured by the Bakewell & Mullins Company of Salem, Ohio. The statue stands on a granite column formed from two pieces of stone which in turn stands on a triple base. On the column above the inscription is a large metal Great Seal of the Confederacy. A circular courtyard of light brown paver stones surrounds the base. A low stone wall of the same color, topped with three sections of metal fence, further outlines the memorial site. Welded into the center fence section is: 1861 CSA 1865. A flag pole with Confederate flag stands left of the monument.

Since its dedication in 1888, the monument has seen several restorations and additions. It was vandalized in 1969 during a period of civil rights unrest and the gun and hand holding it broken off. It was repaired through efforts of Elihu Walker Camp 1290, Sons of Confederate Veterans (SVC). The hand and gun were not recovered and the replacements are of bronze. In 1984, the John Sloan Camp, SCV 1290 led a second restoration and added the second granite column section to raise the statue's height. During Confederate Memorial Day services on May 10, 2008, the Great Seal of the Confederacy was dedicated. Later in 2008 a tree limb fell during a storm causing severe damage to the statue. The John Sloan Camp 1290 also led this restoration effort. Evidence of repairs can be seen on the soldiers back and legs. Erosion of the burial mound forced further modifications to the site and on May 10, 2011 the protective and memorial wall was dedicated. In 2017 the 1888 inscription was extended, noting that the Ladies' Memorial Association, the original sponsor of the monument, was the predecessor to the Guilford Chapter of the Daughters of the Confederacy.

Source: Commemorative Landscapes of North Carolina, https://docsouth.unc.edu/commland/monument/150/

Day 6 at F. W. Woolworth lunch counter in Greensboro, North Carolina, 1960

The nonviolent sit-in during the civil rights movement was a radical act of defiance that exceeds the possibility of photographic representation. Civil rights protesters routinely faced mortal danger at the hands of law enforcement, whether in the form of water cannons, dogs, or arrest, and it was within this state of normalized violence that the "Greensboro Four"—Ezell Blair Jr., David Richmond, Franklin McCain, and Joseph McNeil, young African American students at North Carolina A&T University—staged the first sit-in on February 1, 1960, at the Woolworth's lunch counter. They broke Jim Crow laws, challenged the racist legal system, faced taunts and physical abuse by white patrons, and confronted the threat of being thrown in jail or even the loss of their lives. They took radical action to bring about radical change

On day 6, students from the all-women's Bennett College continued the sit-in at the Woolworth's lunch counter and refused to leave after being denied service. The sit-in movement soon spread to college towns throughout the South.

A monument to honor Wilson County, Tennessee Confederate veterans with their local leader on the pedestal

TITLE: Confederate Monument

ARTIST(S):Unknown

Date Installed or Dedicated: 05/20/1912

Name of Government Entity or Private Organization that built the monument: S.G. Shepard Camp #941 UCV

PHYSICAL LOCATION:
Town Square, S. Cumberland Street

N36°12.480 W86°17.460

Description: In 1861, Robert H. Hatton called for volunteers on Lebanon's Square. Close to one thousand men came to make the march to Nashville to sign up then marched to Camp Trousdale to train. The 7th TN Infantry was then assigned to fight in the Army of Northern Virginia with General Robert E. Lee.

Robert H Hatton was promoted to the rank of General on May 23, 1862. Eight days later he died at the Battle of Seven Pines defending Richmond, Virginia. His men went on to fight in every major battle in the war. When General Lee surrendered at Appomattox Court house, 47 men from the 7th TN Infantry were left. In 1912 this statue of General Hatton was erected on the square in Lebanon. He is buried at Cedar Grove Cemetery along with 125 other confederate heroes.

Around the same time Hatton and the 7th Tennessee were in Virginia, a fierce battle occurred on the square in Lebanon. Col. John Hunt Morgan and his Daring Raiders were in town when Gen. Dumont mounted a surprise attack. Morgan escaped to the east and crossed the Cumberland River at Rome Ferry but lost his trusty steed, Black Bess. This was Morgan's first loss in battle. Several of the men killed in this battle are buried, like General Hatton, at Cedar Grove Cemetery.

Source: http://www.waymarking.com/waymarks/WM28HC_Confederate_Memorial_Lebanon_TN

Police mug shots of Congressman John Lewis, a civil rights movement pioneer.
Seen here are arrests from 1961, right, and 1962, left

As a student at Fisk University, John Lewis organized sit-in demonstrations at segregated lunch counters in Nashville, Tennessee. In 1961, he volunteered to participate in the Freedom Rides, which challenged segregation at interstate bus terminals across the South. Lewis risked his life on those rides many times by simply sitting in seats reserved for white patrons. He was also beaten severely by angry mobs and arrested by police for challenging the injustice of Jim Crow segregation in the South including during the march across the Edmund Pettus Bridge in Selma, Alabama, the day that became known as "Bloody Sunday."

During the height of the civil rights movement, from 1963 to 1966, Lewis was named Chairman of the Student Nonviolent Coordinating Committee (SNCC), which he helped form. SNCC was largely responsible for organizing student activism, including sit-ins and other activities. At the age of 23, he was an organizer and a keynote speaker at the historic March on Washington in August 1963.

*Civil War memorial in front of the Hale County
Courthouse in Greensboro, Alabama*

TITLE: Confederate Monument

ARTIST(S): Unknown Sculptor; Elledge and Norman, fabricator.

DATE: Installed April 26, 1904. Dedicated May 12, 1904.

MEDIUM: Figure: Italian marble; Base: granite.

PHYSICAL LOCATION:

Hale County Courthouse Centerville Street, between Whelan & Main Streets Greensboro, Alabama

Description: The monument has a Confederate soldier standing at parade rest and looking straight forward.
The figure is standing on a tall shaft. The shaft has reliefs of crossed rifles on one side and crossed
sabres on the opposite. The shaft rests on a base with Confederate flag on the front and the names of war
dead on the other three sides.
The monument is inscribed:

(Front)

LEST

WE FORGET

OUR

CONFEDERATE/SOLDIERS.

1861-1865

(On lower base:)

Erected

by

the Ladies Memorial

Association

April 26, 1904

Gov. George C. Wallace stands in the doorway to block integration at the University of Alabama, 1963

George Wallace, first elected governor of Alabama from 1962 said famously in his 1963 inaugural "Segregation now! Segregation tomorrow! Segregation forever!" In June of 1963, Wallace—flanked by state troopers—blocked the door to the enrollment office at the University of Alabama to prevent the integration of the school and the enrollment of Vivian Malone and James A. Hood. Although the U.S. Supreme Court had declared segregation unconstitutional in 1954's Brown v. Board of Education, and the federal executive branch undertook aggressive tactics to enforce the ruling, Wallace stood in defiance.

Then, on June 10, 1963, President John F. Kennedy federalized National Guard troops and deployed them to the University of Alabama to force its desegregation. The following day, Governor Wallace relented to the federal pressure, and the two African American students successfully enrolled.

Orangeburg Confederate Monument, Orangeburg, South Carolina

TITLE: Orangeburg Confederate Memorial

ARTIST(S): Markwalter, T.

DATE: Oct 18, 1893

MEDIUM: bronze, Winnsborogh granite

PHYSICAL LOCATION:
Town Square, 222 Middleton Street S.E.,
Orangeburg, South Carolina 29115

N33°29.412 W80°51.810

Description: Uniformed Confederate soldier stands atop a tall pedestal which rests on a tiered base. The figure faces southwest and leans on his rifle with both hands. A canteen and haversack hang from his proper left shoulder and a knife is at his proper left side. He carries a bedroll and a kepi rests on his head. The model for the sculpture was a Confederate soldier named John S. Palmer.

Inscriptions:

(On north face:)

TO THE CONFEDERATE DEAD OF/ORANGBURG (sic) DISTRICT

(On east face:)

ERECTED BY THE WOMEN OF/ORANGEBURG COUNTY 1893.

(On south face:)

A GRATEFUL TRIBUTE/TO THE BRAVE DEFENDERS OF/OUR RIGHTS/OUR HONOR/AND OUR HOMES

(On west face:)

LET POSTERITY EMULATE THEIR/VIRTUES/AND TREASURE THE/MEMORY OF THEIR/VALOR AND PATRIOTISM

Remarks: The monument was initiated and designed by the Orangeburg Confederate Monument Association and was cast in a small town in Massachusetts. It was moved within the town square when the courthouse where it stood was razed. IAS files include a related article from the Times and Democrat and citations to "History of the Confederate Monument," by Mrs. George Love (Inabinet) Adams, Orangeburg County Librarian, and editorials from the Times and Democrat, Oct. 18, 1893 and Oct. 25, 1893.

Source: http://www.waymarking.com/waymarks/WM9PCO_Orangeburg_Confederate_Monument_Orangeburg_SC

Highway troopers standing over the bodies of murdered students during the Orangeburg Massacre, South Carolina, 1968

The Orangeburg Massacre occurred on the night of February 8, 1968, when a civil rights protest at South Carolina State University (SC State) turned deadly after highway troopers opened fire on about 200 unarmed black student protesters during a demonstration to desegregate the All-Star Triangle Bowling Lanes. Three young men were shot and killed, and 28 people were wounded. The three young men were Samuel Hammond, Henry Smith (both SC State students), and Delano Middleton, who was still in high school at the time. Nine of those troopers faced federal charges, but were acquitted and the FBI refused to reopen an investigation.

The event became known as the Orangeburg Massacre and is one of the most violent episodes of the civil rights movement, yet it remains one of the least recognized.

Confederate monument south of the Old Capitol building, Jackson, Mississippi

TITLE: Confederate Monument

DATE: May 25, 1891

Name of Government Entity or Private Organization that built the monument: United Daughters of the Confederacy & State of Mississippi

PHYSICAL LOCATION:
In front of the Mississippi Department of Archives and History on S State Street in Jackson

Description: This monument was erected 1888-1891 through the combined efforts of the United daughters of the Confederacy and the Mississippi legislature. The cornerstone was laid on May 25, 1888, with Varina "Winnie" Davis, a daughter of Ex-Confederate President Jefferson Davis, in attendance.

Symbolic devices include the traditional Sentinel standing watch on high, 3 marble plaques with crossed muskets, Canon, and shield, the letter CSA, and interior dedicatory plaques with the following inscriptions:

NORTHWEST
God and our consciences alone
Give us measures of right and wrong.
The race may fall to the swift
And the battle to the strong;
But the truth will shine in history
And blossom into song.

SOUTHWEST
The men to whose memory this Monument is dedicated
were martyrs
Of their creed, their justification is in the Holy
Keeping of the God of History

NORTH
Officers of the Confederate Monument Association
of Mississippi
AD 1890
Miss Sally B Morgan, President
Mrs. Belmont Phelps Manship, Vice President
Mrs. Elenor H Stone, Treasurer
Miss Sophie de Langley, Secretary
Mrs. Virginia P. McKay, Cor. Secretary

SOUTH
The noble women of Mississippi, moved by grateful hearts and loving zeal, organized June 15, A.D. 1886, the Confederate Monument Association. Their efforts, aided by an appropriation of the state of Mississippi, were crowned with success in the erection of this Monument to the Confederate dead of Mississippi, in the year 1891.

NORTHEAST
"All lost! But by the graves
Where martyred heroes rest.
He wins the most who honor saves
Success is not the test."

SOUTHEAST
"It recks not where the bodies lie."
By bloody hillside, plain, or river.
Their names are bright on Fame's proud sky.
Their deeds of valor live forever.
Decoration Day
Originated in Jackson Mississippi
April 26, 1865.
By Sue Landon Vaughn

Cornerstone inscription:
Laid by the Grand Lodge of Masons, M. M. Evans, Grand Master. May 25, A. D. 1888

Source: http://www.waymarking.com/waymarks/WMWD72_Mississippi_Confederate_Monument_Jackson_MS

"The Tougaloo Nine" are escorted from the Jackson Public Library, 1961

In March of 1961, the "Tougaloo Nine" entered the largest library in Jackson, Mississippi, in order to desegregate the library. They sat quietly at different tables reading books that are not available in the "colored" library. When the nine refused to leave, they are arrested for "Disturbing the Peace" and were jailed for 36 hours.

Death at Jackson State. From left, Senator Walter F. Mondale of Minnesota, Carl Griffin, a student, and Senator Birch Bayh of Indiana survey the scene, 1970

On May 14, 1970, around 9:30 pm, a group of African American high school and college students gathered just off campus and began rioting in response to a false rumor that Fayette, Mississippi, Mayor Charles Evers, the brother of slain civil rights activist Medgar Evers, and his wife at the time, Nannie Evers, were assassinated. Several white motorists called Jackson Police Department to complain about the African American rioters throwing rocks at them as they drove by the campus on Lynch Street. Seventy-five policeman and Mississippi State Police officers responded to the call, arriving to control the crowd. Around 12:05 a.m. on May 15, 1970, the police opened fire at the crowd and killed four and wounded twelve.

CHAPTER 3

NO LAND
BEEYOND

Lake Michigan, Chicago, 2019. Photo: Cover Images / Associated Press

In early 2019 the polar vortex brought the coldest weather in decades to the midwestern United States. In Chicago large portions of Lake Michigan were frozen, and the city was virtually stalled for more than two days. The impacts of what has been called a "lethal cold" were felt most severely by the city's homeless population, and warming shelters were established throughout Chicago. Scientists have established a strong link between warming Arctic temperatures and severe winter weather in the American Northeast and Midwest. In this age of global climate emergency, extreme weather events of this kind and their devastating social and economic impacts are likely to become the new normal.

FOREST FOR THE TREES

EDUARDO KOHN

"ECOLOGIZING" ETHICS

We are living in an age of unprecedented anthropogenic climate change, that much is clear. It has also become apparent that our human-centered ethical frameworks—those that orient our conduct, dictate our norms, inform our core values, and ultimately allow us to imagine a better way of life—are inadequate to the challenges humanity faces. The task before us is to radically rethink just what it means to be human and to reimagine how to conduct our lives on a planet we share with the vast but fragile web of life of which we are a part. Grasping the magnitude and urgency of this task demands that we develop the conceptual equipment—the ideas and methods—to create a form of ethics that goes beyond the human. We need, in short, to "ecologize" ethics. Given our scholarly traditions, which continue to treat ethical questions as strictly human affairs, and our political traditions, which still equate the good with unfettered human progress, this is a daunting challenge.

Such an "ecologized" ethics would build on the "green ethics" that emerged with the environmental movement of the 1970s. That movement focused largely on the important task of finding a better way to act toward nature, but our current times require something else: that we derive an ethics from the ways nature acts on us. For we are now seeing the planetary effects of seemingly unconstrained human agency. This demands an ethics that inverts the terms of the agential relationship. The challenge is not so much to actively apply an ethics to ecology but rather to listen patiently and learn how an ethical practice can be derived from the ecological relations that hold us.

THE WORK OF DESIGN

This challenge forces me to rethink my vocation, anthropology—the study of what it means to be human. For it asks me to consider the human not by virtue of what is distinctive to it but with a view to that which lies beyond it and sustains it. This shift in perspective has in turn led me, perhaps unexpectedly, to think about "design." That is, it has led me to think about the centrality of configurations of regularity, form, and pattern as constraints on possibility; the ways in which such configurations inform action, human and otherwise; and how a reflection on such configurations, which I take to be the central task of design thinking,

1.

Eduardo Kohn, *How Forests Think: Toward an Anthropology beyond the Human* (Berkeley: University of California Press, 2013).

2.

Gregory Bateson, *Steps to an Ecology of Mind* (Chicago: University of Chicago Press, 2000).

decenters the expected human locus of agency and thus what it means to be human. Finding, as I believe we must, a way to orient our conduct by opening ourselves to the pattern-propagating network of living relations impels us to question how we work with design or, more to the point, how we allow designs not of our making to work on us.

To move toward a better way of living requires a "move" back, so to speak, to a recognition of the form or pattern that can "inform" that movement. Another way to put this is that an ecologized ethics finds its guidance by attuning itself to the emergent aesthetic background that life itself both generates and makes manifest. The task of what I would call a "design-oriented anthropology" is to understand the connection between aesthetics and ethics—between the appreciation of something spatial (a form) and something temporal (an action toward an end)—as central to the development of methods and practices that will allow us to discern possibility in the forms that hold us.

ECOLOGIES
OF MIND

Thinking ethics ecologically requires that we rethink what we mean by thought. We tend to think of thought as something exclusively human. There is, of course, a distinctively human way of thinking. It involves the emergence of a virtual system of signs that refer indirectly to the world. The word *dog*, for example, is a sign that refers indirectly to the furry four-legged creature by virtue of its relation to other words in English, such as *cat*, or classes of words, such as nouns.

This kind of sign process, termed *symbolic*, gives human thought distinctive properties. We can think about things that are quite separate from our experiences—extraterrestrials, 1492, climate change—and we can conjure them, reflect on them, negate them, and even be aware that we are doing so.

The social sciences emerged in an effort to grasp the special kind of reality that this kind of thinking engenders. They allow us to appreciate the ways in which human life is held and fixed by cultural meanings and social structures. But they give us very little understanding of the ways in which this kind of thought relates to a world beyond the symbolic realm. The root cause of our planetary crisis—with all its ecological, social, and political reverberations—is a tendency for humans to see ourselves as separate from the world and to act in ways that further this separation. So an understanding of human thought that emphasizes only its autonomy from the rest of life gets in the way of the kind of ethics we need.

There exists, however, a larger arena of thought that holds the symbolic, a kind of thinking that, when we recognize it as thought in its own right, allows us to think in a different way. As I argue in *How Forests Think*, a book based on immersive fieldwork in Ecuador's upper Amazon, in order truly to comprehend what it means to live in these times of anthropogenic climate change, we need to reimagine our relationship to a larger living world that truly—but in sometimes counterintuitive ways—also thinks.[1] To do so, I develop a conceptual tool kit and

Fig. 1
Chocó rainforest, Ecuador, 2017

a set of alternative ethnographic methods based on semiotics, the study of signs, to understand this kind of thinking-beyond-the-human and its relation to human thought in ways that can overcome the kinds of separations symbolic thought engenders.

Although we tend to see human thought—associated with language, consciousness, and brains—as the only kind of thought worthy of the name, semiotics gives us the technical tools to trace the formal continuities between human and nonhuman thought. It thus helps us appreciate the profound connection we have with the rest of life—namely, that we all think through representational processes that involve signs, not all of which are symbolic. This connection, then, is not based on the fact of our shared physicality. If what we share with other kinds of beings is not so much our bodies but our *minds*, then how we think—and especially what we think—can be informed by what Gregory Bateson called the larger "ecology of mind," of which our individual human minds are just a part.[2]

THE SHAPE OF THOUGHT

Our distinctive kind of thinking is nested within a larger nonhuman semiotic dynamic that we humans share with the rest of the living world. This dynamic is not symbolic and hence not language-like and is made up of semiotic processes that involve two other kinds of signs: icons, or imagistic signs of likeness—such as those involved in the ways the Amazonian katydid *Cycloptera speculata* has, over the course of evolutionary time, come to look

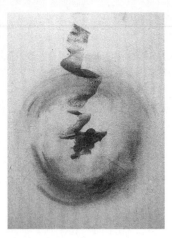

Fig. 2
Eduardo Kohn, *Finding a direction in a shape*, 1999

Fig. 3
Translating the forest's thoughts into legal idioms. The Sarayaku technical team discusses their Living Forest proposal, Facultad Latinoamericana de Ciencias Sociales, Quito, 2016

Fig. 4
Finding a direction in the forest's spirit life. Healing with tobacco among the Sápara Nation, Ecuador, 2017

like the leaves around it—and indices, which point to something, such as a monkey's cry that indicates danger.

Iconic thought has a "shape." That is, there is a holistic closure to it. Think of that leaflike Amazonian katydid. It doesn't exactly refer to the leaf; it is simply "leafy" and is thus complete, in and of itself, regardless of any leaves that may or may not be part of its environment.

But thought also has a "direction," insofar as it refers to anything other than itself (and reference of course is the "end" of thought). That direction emerges from a "shape." This is visible, for example, in the ways in which we might learn to take smoke to be an index of fire. An instance of smoke iconically recalls prior experiences of smoke and their associations with fire. Memories of smoke and fire, in turn, iconically and effortlessly become associated with other such memories to the point that the current instance of smoke compels us to complete the icon by searching for the missing fragment—the fire beyond our purview—that would make the thought whole.[3]

This is an example of how directional thinking emerges from a kind of form thinking in a way that involves design. That is, I take the task of design to be concerned with accessing the "shape of thought" in ways that can orient the directionality of thought as a means of ecologizing our ethics.

FOREST FOR THE TREES

If I could capture in one phrase this ambition to ecologize ethics by virtue of an immersion in form,

3.
This example is drawn from Terrence Deacon, *The Symbolic Species* (New York: Norton, 1997).

4.
Charles Peirce, "Pragmatism as the Logic of Abduction" (1903), in *The Essential Peirce: Selected Philosophical Writings: Volume 2, 1893–1913* (Bloomington: Indiana University Press, 1998), 226–41.

that phrase would be "forest for the trees." The old adage about being unable "to see the forest for the trees" alludes to the common-enough failure of the human imagination to abstract from the particular. I invoke and tweak it here to point to a failure of a different order: namely, our failure to recognize the ways in which a forest is actually greater than the sum of its individual parts. A "forest," then, is not just a human abstraction we impose on a world supposedly made up exclusively of so many "trees." Rather the general or abstract quality of a forest is—just like the "leafiness" expressed by an Amazonian katydid—an emergent property that dense living semiotic assemblages intrinsically come to manifest. That is, a forest *qua* forest manifests thought and is not just the product of our thinking. Furthermore, such a forest exhibits some of the properties of thinking—such as end-directedness and generalization—that we tend to associate exclusively with humans.

If this is so, then it behooves us to learn to listen for what such thinking can express and, as strange as this may sound, to recognize the ways in which the *forest* can provide a kind of ethical orientation *for* the sake of the various human and nonhuman life forms—the *trees*, so to speak—it sustains.

Learning to recognize an emergent general whole such as a "forest" is another instance of developing technologies of thought by which design can work on us. It turns on learning how to appreciate what the philosopher Charles Peirce termed "abduction." This refers to the mental process by which we suddenly recognize a general conception that makes sense of seemingly fragmented parts. An abduction involves the spontaneous emergence of a new thought—a guess, a hypothesis, a theory.[4] Abductions, crucially, cannot be willed. Like whirlpools they must emerge. And we, like riverbeds, can create only the conditions of receptivity—the appropriate geometries of constraint—that allow them to take form. They exemplify a kind of thinking that involves moving forward by falling back into a "shape." They are intimations of the way a design can emerge without a designer.

TOPOLOGY OF THE GOOD

Just how to discern such guidance from the holistic properties that a living world manifests is a complex philosophical problem that turns on, as Plato long ago intimated, the relation between aesthetics and ethics. Between, that is, form and some sort of consideration of intention that is directionally guided—"informed," as it were—by form. The task of design thinking is to grasp this connection and learn to work with it.

As with icons and abductions, this too involves learning to recognize the "shapes" that hold us. Recall the example of smoke. As an index it points to something new—fire!—by "completing" the holistic topology or image of the icon; we can now see smoke as pointing to the fire that would make it part of a whole. Similarly, what Peirce termed an abduction—"Oh, this is a forest!"— subsumes fragments (the trees) under a larger whole.

5.
Charles Peirce, "The Three Normative Sciences" (1903), in *Essential Peirce*, 2:201.
6.
Richard Powers, *The Overstory* (New York: Norton, 2018), 454.

For Peirce ethics involves a similar process by which one discerns from a topology an "end" or orientation that will dictate appropriate action in the world. Underlying and informing the ethical good, he argues, is a more basic kind of good, which he calls the aesthetic good. The aesthetic good involves the ways in which our experience of the world results in a kind of end that is a feeling. For him the aesthetic good has a formal or topological quality to it. That is, it has a "shape." He writes: "An object, to be aesthetically good, must have a multitude of parts so related to one another as to impart a positive simple immediate quality to their totality."[5]

Ethics emerges from aesthetics because, as a higher-order emergent thought process in its own right, it is itself grounded in the ways in which indices emerge from icons. A forest, understood as a vast and multilayered ecology of mind, expresses all these emergent properties as well as their continuities with those dynamics that sustain them. This is why learning to attend to how we humans are continuous with its kind of thought is so central to cultivating an ethics that is ecological.

WILD GUESSES

How an ethics can emerge from the holistic properties of something like a forest is not just a question to be studied from the academic armchair. It is also a question that a diverse Ecuadorian network of Indigenous activists, academics, scientists, lawyers, architects, and artists is exploring in the real world as part of their own innovative experiment in philosophical speculation aimed at finding a better way of life for our times. My own anthropological speculations about "ecologizing" ethics are grounded in that context— that "ecology of mind." They emerge from close collaborations with these actors in sites ranging from United Nations forums to museums, law schools, frontier towns, and remote rain forests. As such—and this is a crucial point—they are eminently empirical, as well as political, even if they are also metaphysical. They have as their goal to take this wild guess—that the forest can serve as a font of ethical guidance for us "trees"—into the wider world.

If my empirical-philosophical speculation draws on a form of speculation already in the everyday world as practiced by these various actors with whom I am collaborating, this is only because that everyday world is itself informed by the kind of speculation that can be found in the kind of world called a forest. One of the characters in Richard Powers's novel *The Overstory* puts it this way: "Trees are doing science. Running a billion field tests. They make their conjectures, and the living world tells them what works. Life is speculation and speculation is life. What a marvelous word! It means to guess. It also means to mirror."[6]

Life itself is a kind of speculation. It involves a series of "wild guesses" about the world in a special way that gets at the double meaning of speculation: speculations about possible futures are guesses—end-directed "abductions," to use Peirce's term—that emerge from a kind of form-directed mirroring, reflection, or patterned iteration of

Fig. 5
Leaf Katydid (*Cycloptera speculata*) camouflaged on leaf, Yasuni National Park, Amazon rain forest, Ecuador, 2011. Photo: Pete Oxford / MINDEN PICTURES

a shape. Learning how to make good "wild guesses," to speculate in a way that finds a direction of movement in the shape of a forest's thoughts, is the work of design.

CODA (A DESIGN NOT OF OUR MAKING)

Amazonians derive an ethical orientation from the forms that a forest generates by cultivating technologies of access—such as dreaming—that allow them to apprehend the forest in its generality or, in the Amazonian idiom, as it manifests itself in its spirit form. Dream interpretation is a way of guiding ethical action by recourse to the more general, holistic, aesthetic, or spirit form from which it emerges. This is possible thanks to the particular iconic logic of dream thinking. In this sense dreams think the way forests think, that is, in a register that is imagistic in nature, one that draws on the holistic properties of icons. Thinking in icons has its own kind of topological causality: one must learn to fall into a dream the way one falls into a form. This makes my anthropological fieldwork a kind of form work—one that seeks to be attuned to an emergent design not of our making as a way to channel a spirit guidance that can manifest itself in the dense ecologies of selves that hold and make each and every one of us.

In our collective dreams perhaps we can learn to see the forest for the trees, to listen for what its thoughts—manifested as spirit—have to say and to act accordingly. If I, along with my Amazonian colleagues, were to venture a wild guess, it would be that this is what we need today.

Cutover field in Michigan, n.d. Courtesy Archives of Michigan

This ghost forest is an image of Chicago—past, present, future. The photograph was taken near the temporary town of Deward, Michigan, and later reproduced in William Cronon's book *Nature's Metropolis: Chicago and the Great West* (1991). It shows the sacrificial landscape left behind by the lumber magnate David Ward, whose vast timber holdings were swiftly liquidated by his heirs after his death in 1900. From the mid-nineteenth to the early twentieth century, majestic stands of white pine across the Great Lakes region were cut, milled, and transported by ship or rail to wholesale lumberyards along the Chicago River's South Branch. The wood—in combination with a newfangled

invention, the steel-wire nail—was used to build the "balloon frame" houses of the city, but much greater volumes were sold to homesteaders across the treeless expanse of the Great Plains. The ghost forest, sprawling market, and commercial hinterland together exemplify the role of metropolitan centers in literally uprooting, absorbing, transforming, and redistributing the basic components of the living world, in the process of global ecological change now called the Anthropocene. There are no more lumberyards along the South Branch; nor are there any significant white pine forests in the Great Lakes region. But the financial derivatives markets that emerged from Chicago's commercial past still govern extractive operations across the earth.
—Brian Holmes

ADVENTURE IN CHINATOWN 1958

My father was a steel worker in Skokie Illinois.
   He would leave before dawn and return long after the
      sun no one ever saw in Chicago went down.

My mother says the buildings were too tall and the air
   stank.
   The only place I went was church, she remembers.

My brother Barry was a month old, making me nothing
   but
   a nagging worry in my mother's mind.
   No more babies she thought
   after the third child
   after the fourth child
   after the fifth child
   and the sixth child.

My father's hunting fed his family
   and his mother's family
   and his brother's family.

People still wonder why he agreed to the
   government relocation program and
   without my mother's consent
   took his Yupik family to Chicago.

In those days they paid the expenses to move
   Native folk out of Native neighborhoods
   and into Asian ones.

It would save them from the mistake
   of the reservation
   would solve the problem
   of that persistent Native identity.

My sister used to take all her clothes off
   and run about naked –
   that's everyone's favorite Chicago story.

106 Susie Silook, "Adventure in Chinatown 1958," *Alaska Quarterly Review: Alaska Native Writers, Storytellers & Orators: The Expanded Edition* 17, nos. 3 and 4 (1999): 252–53. Courtesy Susie Silook

My other sister got lost and only spoke Yupik
   and so they took her all over Chinatown
   looking for her non-existent Asian family.

Someone must have told them
   that child is not Asian for
   she remembers eating ice cream at the
   precinct and my father remembers
   how big her eyes were when he
   came to claim his
   relocated but not indigenous to
   Chinatown girl.

Mrs. Silook, why do you want to poison your children?
   the psychiatrist asked my mother.

My father would repeat day in and day out
   Sakuuma paneghaallequusi
   You will all starve if something happens to me.

Finally my Iñupiaq-Irish mother who spoke only Yupik
   shouted
   Then we should buy poison and prepare ourselves!

My father wouldn't go to work unless
   she stayed up all night to watch everyone.

The woman was *tired* you got that?

I didn't mean it, she told the lady,
   I was tired of Saavla saying we were going to starve.

So, Custer's Last Stand II
   or infinity
   lasted one month
   in Chinatown.

Better to starve as a Yupik than as impossible immigrant
   read the fortune cookie of my father
   who says only that
   Chicago is too big to remember.

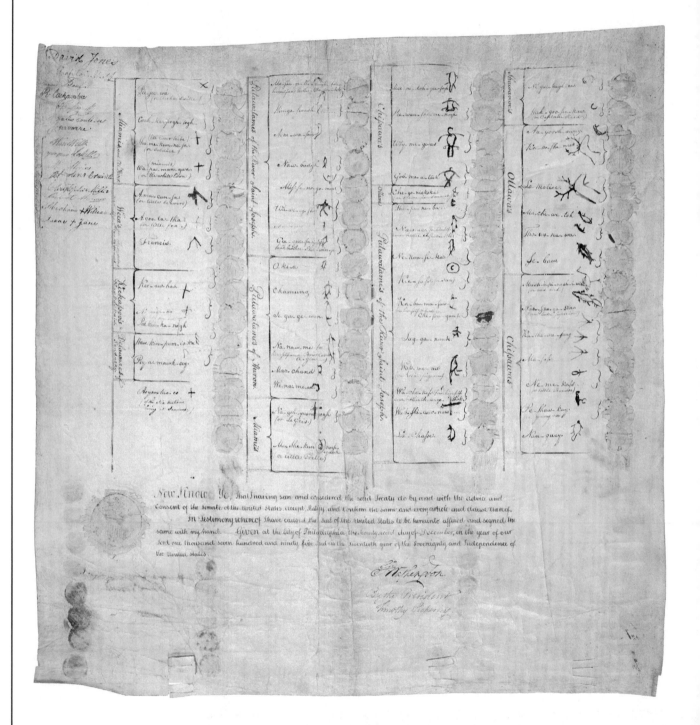

Now Know Ye, That I having seen and considered the said Treaty do by and with the advice and consent of the senate of the united states accept, ratify and confirm the same and every article and clause thereof. In Testimony whereof I have caused the seal of the united states to be hereunto affixed and signed the same with my hand. Given at the City of Philadelphia the twenty second day of December, in the year of our Lord one thousand seven hundred and ninety five and in the twentieth year of the sovereignty and Independence of the united states

G. Washington

By the President
Timothy Pickering

Signature page from the Treaty of Greenville (Ratified Indian Treaty #23, 7 STAT 49), which ended the Indian War on the Northwest frontier, 1795. Courtesy National Archives, Washington, DC

At the Battle of Fallen Timbers (1794), a confederacy of Indians organized by the leaders Blue Jacket (Shawnee) and Little Turtle (Miami) was defeated near Maumee, Ohio. The following year the tribes of the Great Lakes tried to ensure peace with the United States by signing the Treaty of Greenville (1795). The final page includes the names of the Indian leaders and signatories. In that treaty much of what is now Ohio was ceded to the United States. The treaty established a temporary peace between the United States and the American Indian tribes that lived in the region but encouraged non-Native immigration to the area. Federal government officials promised the Native leaders that they would be treated fairly in future dealings. Article 5 of the treaty specifically provided that the Indians would retain the right to quietly enjoy their lands until and unless sold to the United States.

Signing on behalf of the Wyandot, Delaware, Shawnee, Ottawa, Miami, Eel River, Wea, Chippewa, Potawatomi, Kickapoo, Piankashaw, and Kaskaskia nations were twenty-three leaders. Those tribes would, in later years, either flee north into the upper Midwest and Canada or be removed west of the Mississippi River pursuant to the 1830 Indian Removal Act, as Ohio became a great scatter zone of ethnic cleansing and diaspora. While the treaty itself is evidence of the intent of the settlers of European descent to wrest the lands away from the first peoples of the region, the document also reflects the cosmopolitan nature of Indigenous life and community in the number of tribes and signatories involved and their desire for peaceful coexistence.

The treaty also provided for the establishment of several American forts, including one at the mouth of the Chicago River. This would represent the first cession of lands by Indian peoples of the Chicago area. Fort Dearborn would be built at this location and become a site of both trade and conflict. The fort was burned by the Potawatomi and other tribes in 1812, but the settlers returned shortly thereafter and by 1833, only thirty-eight years after the Treaty of Greenville, the Treaty of Chicago ceded the last of the Chicago region. In one lifetime the Indigenous peoples of what is now Chicago had been hustled out of town.

—John N. Low

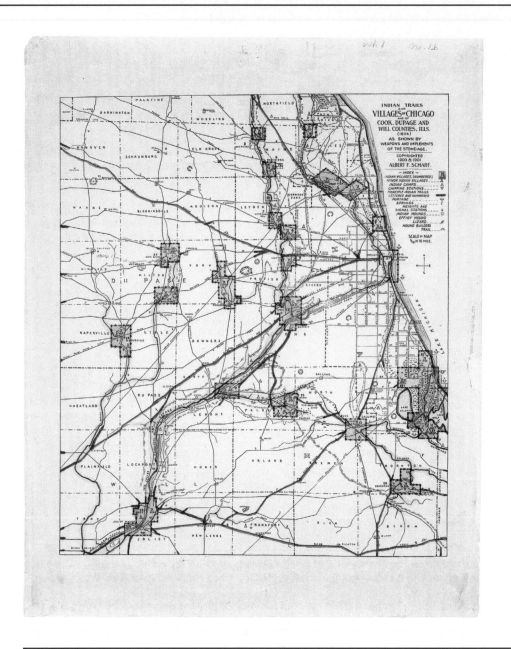

Albert F. Scharf, Indian Trails and Villages of Chicago as Shown by Weapons and Implements of the Stone Age, ca. 1804, ca. 1900. Courtesy Chicago History Museum (ICHi-029629)

Beginning in 1900 the surveyor and amateur cartographer Albert F. Scharf mapped the villages and trails of the Indigenous peoples of the area that is now Chicago as they existed around 1804. Mapmaking has a long tradition in the Western world. Nonindexical, maps theoretically need no additional information to provide context; they are regarded as scientific and therefore unbiased and beyond dispute. The truth is that mapmaking was an essential part of the colonial project. First the settlers mapped the land with a system of lines, metes, and bounds, drawing it so that it was recognizable to them, and then they claimed it and divvied it up. Scharf's map represents the last step of this process: once the settler-colonists had displaced the Indigenous peoples of the area, they nostalgically traced their presence as a sort of cultural patrimony and curiosity.

Ironically the map itself subverts the standard colonial attempt at erasure by providing evidence of the long-standing and extensive human habitation of the region. Scharf based his map on "the weapons and implements of the stone age." The subtext of the map is that Indians were primitive peoples of the past. His map gives no hint that Simon Pokagon, a Potawatomi leader, had spoken before an audience of seventy thousand people at the World's Columbian Exposition in Chicago in 1893 or that the Potawatomi were making a claim to the Chicago lakefront that by 1917 would end in the US Supreme Court. No, Scharf's map ignores these inconvenient complexities and celebrates Indians in a safe way—through the gaze of a map.

—John N. Low

UNCEDED TERRITORY: HISTORICIZING VANCOUVER

SEPAKE ANGIAMA, CHEYANNE TURIONS, AND VINCENT TAO

Vincent Tao is a labor union organizer, housing activist, and educator focusing on the history and practice of social movements. As a curator, cultural worker, and writer, cheyanne turions responds to artistic practices by linking aesthetics and politics through discourse. Here Sepake Angiama speaks to Tao and turions—both based in Vancouver, Canada— about how to inhabit and historicize a place. They discuss what it means to live in a city acknowledged as unceded territory, exploring questions of colonialism, Indigenous sovereignty, gentrification, and climate change.

SEPAKE ANGIAMA: In our research for the Chicago Architecture Biennial, we began by looking at the narrative of Chicago. How did we come to this city next to Lake Michigan, this place we now call Chicago? How is this narrative told by Chicagoans themselves, and how is it manifested in the city? One of the first places that we visited was the Newberry Library, which holds many maps of Chicago. Chicago has probably been one of the most mapped cities in the world, partly because of the Chicago School and the kinds of maps they created and also because, I believe, it was seen at one point as a frontier city. So there is this notion of a constant expansion to the west and a constant colonization of land, which, through treaties, increasingly displaced people.

It was interesting to come to Vancouver for our research initiative "(un)Learning Geography" in January 2019. It is a city that sits on the edge of the land that we call Canada today. This prompted us to consider notions of western expansion and colonization of land as well as recognition of what it means to be situated on territory that is recognized as illegally occupied. We wanted to consider what it actually means for lived experience in the city and what it means in terms of the practice of architecture, specifically for those with an indigenous relationship to the land. I wanted to start off by asking, what does the notion of treaty mean in the context of Vancouver today, considering that it is acknowledged as unceded territory?

CHEYANNE TURIONS: There is a general practice in Canada of doing territorial acknowledgments at events. Facilitators will name the traditional territories that the events are situated on, sometimes by naming Indigenous nations, sometimes by naming the numbered treaties that were signed between Indigenous nations and the Canadian state as part of colonial settlement. With good intentions, the practice recognizes historical context as connected to present realities (although in practice the acknowledgments are often performative only, at best). The treaties were meant to structure mutually beneficial relationships between the Canadian state and Indigenous nations, but in fact they have been used as tools of colonial dispossession.

In Vancouver there are no treaties, so there was never even this symbolic gesture of formalizing a relationship between a colonizing force and the Indigenous populations that have existed here since time immemorial. It is a fact that the lands of this city were stolen outright and that the city's life is lived as or under a condition of occupation for most of the people who call this place home.

It's strange that we point to treaties when we do territorial acknowledgments because the treaties represent a relationship between the state and Indigenous people, commemorating a moment of colonial encounter through treaty making. I worry that pointing to treaties becomes a way of trying to absolve settler populations that live in these places from grappling with the fact that settler colonialism is an ongoing structure, that settler colonialism is not undone in a moment of treaty making. In practice, treaties have been utilized to displace, dispossess, and disempower Indigenous people, not to recognize their sovereignty or honor their cultures.

VINCENT TAO: Treaties also have a flattening effect on the complex, contested relationships of Indigenous leadership structures. Canada's elected chief and council system was installed by the colonial regime through the Indian Act of 1876. Recent pipeline conflicts on Indigenous land have dramatized a generations-long struggle between elected chiefs who approved the construction and hereditary chiefs who opposed it, the latter belonging to a traditional form of leadership passed down through kinship.

The question of precisely who is bound by a treaty—whether it's between the state and Indigenous people or between the state and a state-installed Indigenous power structure—needs to be complicated.

SA   Yes, it's quite interesting to complicate the narrative or break down the relationship between the parties or the active agents that we consider when we think of an agreement between people. At least in the context of Chicago, a treaty is definitely understood as something that separates the Indigenous people of that place and the colonial settlers. I want to add another element, which is the narrative that the first settler in the area that is now Chicago was Jean Baptiste Point du Sable, who was a black Haitian man who had integrated into the communities that were living there and had a very prominent abode, where he was trading with different groups of people in the area. And actually shortly after the Treaty of Greenville, he moved to another location.

But I'm intrigued by the question of why this narrative is so prominent, why it is told so much, and I think it has partly to do with the idea that he was a free man, a black man but also a colonial body. So when we're looking at this today, what does that mean? That claim to land and that claim to heritage. Does that speak to either of you?

CT   Treaty is a way of forming relationships that predates contact, and I doubt the treaty you're describing was the first that governed relationships in the place now known as Chicago. Maybe it was the first signed with a colonizing force? It is important to recognize that relationships between different Indigenous nations and negotiations about resources—including territory—have being going on forever.

SA   That's an interesting point, actually, because there were different Indigenous groups in Chicago, living in relatively close proximity, forming the Council of Three Fires, characterized as a brotherhood: from the older brother, the Ojibwe; to the middle brother, the Odawa; to the younger brother, the Potawatomi. Each of these tribes also considered themselves keepers or guardians of faith, trade, and fire. Their treaty obviously predates a colonial narrative and is one that's not talked about enough, I think.

CT   Some nations in the part of the world where Chicago is located would have used wampum as a way of recording treaty relationships, reflecting Indigenous legal orders. Wampum is something that lives in the body, that has material form, and it is different from what we usually refer to when discussing treaty today, which is related to colonial legal systems and court documents.

SA   Yes, I often think about this in relation to documents and documentation and also, in a way, all the problematics around the archive. I was recently at an education summit where we were problematizing the archive in relation to women. We were talking about how history is told and how the archive allows for a certain narrative to be told, but we have to be aware of that not being a complete narrative.

In the case of Chicago and, I think, many other geographies, the treaty, as a kind of bodily expression of how a relationship is formed, is something that's passed from person to person but not necessarily in the form of a document.

VT The treaty process also has the effect of erasing or obscuring history, the history of the struggle to resist colonial settlement and imperialism. A treaty is intended to make a moment in history legible—and in the case of the Indian Act, to make a "people" and its relationship to the state legible—but legible according to the logic and the legal grid of the colonial regime. That's what the treaty does: it petrifies and flattens an ongoing history of violence and resistance into a dusty stack of paper. It's important to understand something like a treaty document by excavating what it hides, what it compresses, and what it destroys. You have to read everything beneath the text.

SA How does this add to the complexity of how we read Vancouver as a city today? I've been to Vancouver only two or three times, but one of the things that hits you about the city is how capital investment is being transformed into real estate, particularly the condominiumization of the city. And another is the hard contrast between the Downtown Eastside and other parts of the city. How can we read this complexity? Can we understand it as something that has been a trope of the colonization of land?

VT As cheyanne was saying, colonization is an ongoing process. In a settler-colonial state the frontier always needs to exist as a boundary earmarked as a resource-rich zone where capital is accumulated through the savage dispossession of Indigenous peoples' land and means of subsistence. The geographer Neil Smith wrote about gentrification as a process akin to imperial expansion and conquest, evicting working-class communities from their homes as their neighborhoods are targeted by predatory real estate pioneers. This is the "new urban frontier."

How gentrification is continuous with the ongoing process of colonization is made brutally explicit in Vancouver's Downtown Eastside. The neighborhood has historically been home to low-income residents, many of whom are First Nations people. It is also the epicenter of the city's present and seemingly endless housing, displacement, and homelessness crisis. Indigenous activists fighting the development of the neighborhood, namely leaders from Power of Women and the Vancouver Area Network of Drug Users, see gentrification for what it is: frontier violence and pillage, making profit off the dispossession of Indigenous territory. Canada's history of colonial conquest cannot be separated from today's siege of the Downtown Eastside.

Condominiumization is first and foremost a profit-making enterprise, transforming the homes of the working class into floating banks of capital for the rich. But there's a secondary effect. Visitors to Vancouver encounter a feeling of the city's eternal newness or, put another way, its historical amnesia. That's because everything solid is melted down and rebuilt, constantly. Redevelopment erases architecture as a living document of history. Every sparkling condo requires paving over sites where histories of struggle could otherwise be read, lived in, and carried on by new generations.

CT   I wonder if there is a way to reframe the logic of constant expansion from the sanitizing connotations of frontier development and to talk about it instead as slaughter or displacement or even, more optimistically, a locus of resistance? The idea of the frontier evacuates the murderous politics from the process of taking over land, resources, and life by force. We have a duty to tell and interpret these histories with a clarity of mind that does not retroactively align them with our current politics or practices. This is especially important because these politics and processes still resonate in the present.

SA   I was just going to speak to that. How do you think about a place that is constantly in flux or constantly being constructed? It's not about static narratives. There's this notion that there is an element of destruction and construction in cities; that's almost how they continue to survive in a way. There is a kind of nostalgia related to a built environment that we don't necessarily have, or at least we're increasingly beginning to realize that relationship to ecology, to land, to trees, to things that have been around for much longer than most buildings.

But I suppose it also comes back to the idea of constantly seeing expansion and growth as a necessity, as opposed to looking at it in a much more circular way. These questions very much relate to Indigenous ways of seeing ourselves as guardians, as opposed to constantly seeking forms of extraction, constantly taking from the land in order to serve ourselves. There are questions I'd like to raise, which fall much more within our practices, whether we are educators, activists, architects, curators, or whatever we're doing: How do we dismantle the kinds of language or the ways of thinking about being with land or being with a city? What does it mean if we consider our decision-making only from a human perspective? How do we not privilege a way of life that recognizes wealth, growth, and profit as guiding principles, that reproduces violence and continues to seek and destroy everything else?

VT   I'm thinking now of William Morris, the craftsman and printmaker who lived a second life as a socialist agitator. In his novel *News from Nowhere* [1890], the narrator awakens in a postrevolutionary society in which private property has been abolished. In one chapter he encounters a garden in Trafalgar Square where revolutionists have toppled a statue of Admiral Nelson and planted an apricot orchard in its place.

Kristin Ross offers a brilliant analysis of this utopian gesture in her book *Communal Luxury* [2015]. Trafalgar Square and the statue of Admiral Nelson are monuments to the British Empire, a petrified architecture that organizes the nation and its time along the violent forward arrow of imperial expansion. The gardens and apricot trees grown in their ruins organize space according to a different temporality, returning a place and its people to an organic, rhythmic sense of time and history that is living and must be tended to, stewarded. History here penetrates the present in a circular process.

I don't know what the lesson is! But a question I'm left with is how do we read history—and read history through architecture—in a way that reconstitutes the history of struggle in the present, sees it as a continuous process rather than a settled document that has had its counternarratives crossed out, redacted, and written over by the master's pen?

It's a difficult process because these histories are destroyed through the processes of gentrification and development. It's the labor of countless nameless people who have built our material world, built our cities, yet they are not remembered with monuments like those in Trafalgar Square. These narratives are hidden beneath the monumental, in the spaces we call the everyday, the vernacular. Once we can read these histories, our duty to them—and to the struggles that persist into the present—becomes inescapable.

CT   I wonder if climate collapse is one way to think about the culmination of a history that will no longer remain silent, stylized, or subsumed into colonial and capitalist narratives? The cost of this will continue to be borne unfairly and disproportionately by people who were systemically dispossessed in the creating of these conditions, which are both contemporary and historical. But there is something about the fact that the earth, in and of itself, is a perfect calculator of so many of the things that we have done. And now our debt is due.

This conversation was recorded via Skype between Kassel and Vancouver on March 31, 2019.

PALATAL
GEOGRAPHIES

VIVIEN
SANSOUR

"Let's enjoy a cup of coffee in our kitchen." He squatted down, picked up a twig, and pretended to hold a pot of coffee and pour me a cup. Yakoub and I were not sitting in his parents' house. We were sitting on top of it—literally. In the midst of what looked like a wild mountain full of weeds were the remaining stones of the homes of his village, Iqrit, in the Upper Galilee. "There is only one thing we are allowed to do now—be buried here."

Za'atar, an herb in the oregano family, is a staple of the Palestinian diet. It is commonly believed that za'atar makes you smart and cures many ailments. In the wild, its aroma is so intense that to find it one can just follow the smell.

A journey through these ancient terrains is a culinary voyage into different forageable flavors. Through herbs ranging from nutty, tender *Pistacia palaestina* leaves to wild fennel and *za'atar,* hundreds of Palestinians, like most Indigenous people around the world, have developed long and intimate relationships with their landscape. Their kitchens are infused with aromas that recall their valleys and mountains. But this millennia-long tradition has been illegalized in an attempt at cultural dominance through vegetal transformation. People like Yakoub and Abu Nidal are now seen as criminals in the eyes of a system that has severed them from their ancestral terrains and deemed them "uncivilized" for eating their history rather than abandoning it. The mere process of walking the land and tasting its bounty has become a risky act requiring great bravery.

Foraging for luféteh (wild mustard) leaves, a beloved wintergreen, with Abu Nidal in the village of Al Walejeh. Sixty percent of the community's land has been confiscated for the construction of an "apartheid wall" that effectively severs them from their food sources and disrupts the area's biodiversity. In this image we see the wall as it was being constructed along the mountain. Its completion destroyed more than 160 of Abu Nidal's fruit trees.

The use of legal barriers and military surveillance to prevent people from accessing both communal and private property, along with Israel's construction of colonies and, ultimately, a concrete dividing wall, is rarely considered in terms of its impact on our seasonal food supply. But these strategies have changed the geography of our senses. We once could depend on our sense of smell to identify a bunch of wild thyme, on our sight to identify a hiding wild asparagus shoot, on our taste buds to tell an edible mustard leaf apart from a weed, or on our grandmother's intuitive wisdom to know the medicine that is present beneath our very own feet.

Shakhakha, *the pissing plant, is used in traditional Palestinian medicine to promote urination and the elimination of toxins from the body. The sample above was given to me by Abu Diaa, a farmer in Wadi Fukin village, in 2018. He was shy to tell me its name but then whispered with a smirk, "Don't repeat the name, just know the benefits."*

Foraging traditions have not been the only fatalities as this landscape has been transformed: in the course of eliminating a population, entire villages have been erased. The village of Immwas, featured in these photographs, was demolished in 1967. Its site has been planted over with non-native pine trees that serve to cover the evidence of a once-vibrant agrarian society. In an effort to trace the history of this village, I followed a hand-sketched map that was created from the memories of the people who once inhabited it. Walking in the shade of the tall trees, accompanied by the sounds of dried pine needles tickling the bottoms of my shoes, I found myself uncovering botanical evidence of an imperfect crime. This crime was challenged by the sprouting almond and pomegranate and the sixteen other native varieties of plants. Their seeds could only exist in this terrain today if at some point in history there had been a community that cultivated and devoured their fruits. I thought about this as I sketched bundles of sumac, a plant used profusely in Palestinian cuisine. And I couldn't help but wonder how it is that trees—in this case the non-native pine and the heirloom almond—have in the process of eliminating a people simultaneously become both the victim and the culprit.

A young heirloom almond tree growing from a seed that
has survived the invasion of the non-native pines

A political map of the destroyed village of Immwas, north of Jerusalem

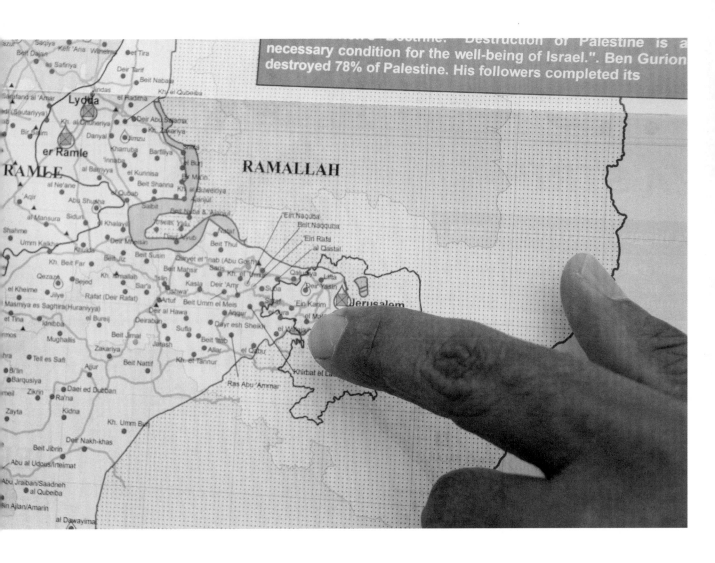

Map of Immwas based on the memories of its people. Dots identify the homes of families that were forced out. To the right are samples of some of the botanical evidence I identified, including carob, sumac, and almonds.

This duality of botanical resilience and violence is seen across the once-familiar topography of Palestine. Ahmed, a farmer from the village of Auja in the Jordan Valley, shows me an image of his sister on their once-lush farm. "Eggplants, tomatoes, watermelons. You name it, we grew it in our little farm. We sold the produce across the West Bank." A farmer turned agribusiness worker who sought employment on settlement date plantations after water was allocated to settlers and cut off from his village, Ahmed says it most accurately: "The valley is now thirsty." He takes me to the top of a mountain where segregation is made starkly visible through a line of symmetrically placed green palm trees that emphasize the thirst felt in the yellow soil alongside them.

Ahmed showing a picture of his sister on their farm before water was cut off and their land turned to desert. "It was a heaven of diversity. It was so abundant people often came to pick and eat for free."

Israeli agribusiness farms in the Jordan Valley have replaced Palestinian sustainable farming, resulting in the desertification of large areas of the valley and transforming Palestinian producers into day laborers on plantations that were once their own farms.

Young Palestinian day laborers on date plantations in the Jordan Valley

Today, organic and foraged foods are experiencing a renaissance in Western markets, and my own practice is similarly revered as "innovative." Yet I stand humbled in front of an old chocolate tin. "I am looking for the heirloom eggplant," I say, in an attempt to entice Om Wisam to open her sacred container that has been emptied to serve as storage for all kinds of ancient seeds. I stare at her collection of zucchini, lettuce, beans, peas, and other heirloom crops that have been slowly disappearing from farmers' hands. In that moment I understand that while the landscape of my ancestors has been deformed, ravished, reformed, and appropriated—much like those pomegranate and almond sprouts in Immwas—I have inherited a resilience that has called me to re-create Om Wisam's Quality Street Mackintosh's chocolate tin in a time of landscape transition. And as I sit in my nicely decorated seed library studio in Battir, a UNESCO World Heritage site, I am interrupted by the blaring of Israeli environmental police sirens on the pine-filled hill across the way. This is the sound of armed officials shoving farmers off their land to make way for natural reserves.

The Jadu'l *watermelon*

The *Jadu'l* watermelon was the seed that sparked my practice of heirloom crop collection. Tens of farmers, elders, and community members I interviewed mentioned this watermelon when recounting personal stories. Some women said they gave birth in the watermelon fields; many men spoke about their fathers and grandfathers loading trucks of *Jadu'l* and taking it to Beirut and Damascus; a woman told me how they used to keep the giant melon under the beds to stay cool so they could eat it in the late autumn. The stories were endless, and the joy in the beaming faces of those talking about this beloved crop was contagious. But when I asked them where the seed of this watermelon was, they said, "You are asking about the dinosaur." A few years later I met Abu Ghattas, a farmer from my hometown, Beit Jala. When I asked him about the *Jadu'l*, he opened his everything drawer full of screwdrivers, nails, and old pieces of paper. He took out a few of the extinct seeds from the chaos of his everything drawer and said, "Here! You are looking for these. Take them. Nobody wants them." The image above is of the first sprouts of the *Jadu'l* seeds in 2016, when we celebrated the vitality of the long-lost crop and affirmed that there are indeed still those who want them—who still want, in essence, who we are!

Samples of my seed collection at a teachers' workshop in Bethlehem

Soil, seed, and water become weapons of war in an environment that is dedicated to a global system of warehousing communities deemed unwanted and seeds deemed unyielding. The ways our terrains have been dominated through lies that make us unfamiliar with ourselves and create a kind of confusion that changes our taste buds, our culture, and our landscape are the most insidious form of control that has been forced on colonized people across the globe. Its rejection is thus the most revolutionary act of all.

CHAPTER 4

COMMON GROUND

133

City Hall, Chicago, 2011. Photo: Charles Rex Arbogast / Associated Press

The City of Chicago maintains beehives in four rooftop locations around the city: two atop City Hall, including the one pictured here; two at Gallery 37; two at Lurie Garden in Millennium Park; and four at the Chicago Cultural Center, a primary venue of the Chicago Architecture Biennial. Cook County is home to more than 1,800 honeybee colonies, many of them managed by civic organizations. Urban initiatives of this kind seek to avert the planetary trend of honeybee die-off caused largely by the massive use of pesticides in global agriculture, a telling indication of the ways anthropogenic-led environmental shifts are driving species extinction and severely impacting the food supply.

THE SCALE OF COMMONS AND SOLIDARITY INFRASTRUCTURES

PELIN TAN

1.
Massimo De Angelis, in
An Architektur, "On the
Commons: A Public
Interview with Massimo De
Angelis and Stavros
Stavrides," e-flux, no. 17
(June 2010), www.e-flux
.com/journal/17/67351
/on-the-commons-a
-public-interview-with
-massimo-de-angelis-and
-stavros-stavrides/.
2.
Alessandro Petti and Sandi
Hillal, "A Common Space
in Fawaar Refugee Camp,"
April 3, 2013, theatrum
-mundi.org/library
/lorem-ipsum/?pdf=165.
See also Alessandro Petti,
"Architecture as Exile,"
in Adhocracy Athens: From
Making Things to Making
the Commons, ed. Ethel
Baraona Pohl, Pelin Tan,
and César Reyes Nájera
(Barcelona: dpr-barcelona;
Athens: Onassis Cultural
Center, 2015), 103–4.

How do we build the commons? How do we create the basis for commoning practices in architecture and design? How do displacement, migration, and contested spaces affect the notion of the commons? According to Massimo De Angelis, "Commons are a means of establishing a new political discourse that builds on and helps to articulate the many existing, often minor, struggles, and recognizes their power to overcome capitalist society."[1] He defines three notions in order to explain the commons not merely in terms of the resources that we share but as a way of commoning, that is, a social process of "being common." It is the way in which resources are pooled and made available to a group of individuals, who then build or rediscover a sense of community.

Spaces where commoning practices are developed in relation to design and architecture are often related to physical spaces in the realm of social design. The ultimate role of spatial design is that the physical structure or form at any scale should serve the practice of commons. Commoning practices require a social assembly process, however, including common decision-making and noncapitalist accumulation; thus it is difficult to develop a consistent design program. The dilemma in design and architecture is rooted in the question of whether an existing act such as squatting in an abandoned building is also a practice of architecture or design. For some architects and designers, even a self-organized refugee camp that has gone through several "intifadas" can be a space of commoning that can inform us about design and architecture. The Palestine-based collective Decolonizing Architecture Art Residency (DAAR) uses the term al masha (communal land) instead of commons: "Masha is shared land, which was recognized through practice in the Islamic world . . . . Masha could only exist if people decided to cultivate the land together. The moment they stop cultivating it, they lose its possession. It is possession through a common use."[2] DAAR uses al masha as a practice of commoning as direct participation and common taking care of life.

In my experience, practices and discourses on commons vary according to scale and territorial specificity. Space-based solidarity practice is one part of practicing the commons; others span from the urban to the rural at different scales. Here the question of scale is not only a physical

3.
Kathryn Yusoff, "Politics of the Anthropocene: Formation of the Commons as a Geologic Process," *Antipode* 50, no. 1 (2017): 272.

4.
Stavros Stavrides, *Common Space: The City as Commons* (London: Zed, 2016), 433–34.

5.
Maribel Casas-Cortés, Sebastian Cobarrubias, and John Pickles, "The Commons," in *A Companion to Urban Anthropology*, ed. Donald M. Nonini (Chichester, UK: Wiley-Blackwell, 2014), 460.

6.
"Refugee Accommodation Center City Plaza," posted April 22, 2016, solidarity2refugees.gr /refugee-accomodation -center-city-plaza.

7.
Wikipedia, s.v. "European Union–Turkey relations," last modified March 24, 2019, 14:25, en.wikipedia .org/wiki/European _ Union%E2%80 %93 Turkey_relations.

8.
Loukia Kotronaki, Olga Lafazani, and Giorgos Maniatis, "Living Resistance: Experiences from Refugee Housing Squats in Athens," *South Atlantic Quarterly* 117 (October 1, 2018): 892.

9.
Refugee Accommodation Space City Plaza, "Open Letter to Ms. Aliki Papachela," April 25, 2017, solidarity2refugees.gr /open-letter/.

element of design and architecture but also reflects how it is *politically conceived*.[3] Stavros Stavrides echoes this argument, as does DAAR, in defining how common space and its structure are important. For Stavrides, "common space shapes commoning practices as well as the subjects of commoning."[4] Common space is relational and relative. I propose that the relationality and relativity of a common space plays a role in the politically conceived scales of how we practice and negotiate with commoning.

The occupation by squatters of a hotel building in Athens that went through a bankruptcy during the recent economic crisis in Greece is an example of how a building designed to function as a hotel can serve as refugee housing as well as a common place, a *masha*. Squatting is a radical practice of starting commoning: "Its contribution to the practice of commoning is its tactical irreverence towards private property, one of the main threats to the commons, especially with the growing wave of privations."[5] The creation of a space-based solidarity action at the Hotel City Plaza in Athens was initiated by refugee families and Greek activists: "In 2015 we witnessed how Greece was brought to its knees through not only the economic crisis characterized by bankruptcy and limited access to resources but also [as it became] one of the main transportation hubs of Syrian and [other] refugees."[6]

The squatting by Greek activists of the Solidarity Initiative for Economic and Political Refugees and by refugee families was a necessity after the announcement of the agreement between the European Union and Turkey in March 2016 to limit the flow of migrants entering the EU through Turkey. Under the terms of the deal Turkey received financial aid and in exchange agreed that all "irregular migrants" (i.e., those who had not gone through the asylum process) crossing from Turkey into Greece would be sent back. Each arrival would be individually assessed by the Greek authorities. The deal was widely criticized, as it appeared to treat migrants as exchangeable subjects for the sake of political advantage (since there was also an offer of renewed consideration of Turkey's bid to join the EU).[7] This caused a huge crisis in Greece: "The tens of thousands of refugees who were about to cross the Greek-Macedonian borders found themselves trapped in Greece, homeless or 'semi-housed,' crowded into awful conditions, in camps, athletic fields, airports, and ports, and facing extreme poverty and a lack of basic amenities."[8] Many self-organized refugee solidarity groups based in Athens and the Greek islands were offering immediate aid to arrivals and spaces to host those who crossed the border from Turkey. This situation also created conflict between the Greek government, Frontex (the European Border and Coast Guard Agency), and the refugee activists.

On my visits to the City Plaza, as I helped to cook meals in the kitchen and mingled with the youth at its café, I was able to witness the activists and the refugees as they went through several negotiations and resolved conflicts. Running the space autonomously in the anarchist tradition of an occupied place

Fig. 1
Residents on a balcony at City Plaza hotel, Athens. Photo: City Plaza Collective

Fig. 2
The key cabinet in the occupied City Plaza hotel, Athens. Photo: City Plaza Collective

with refugees of many different nationalities and ethnic and religious identities is a challenging endeavor. Besides fighting against private ownership; resisting the threats of far right, nationalist, and racist neighbors; and managing donations and volunteers, there are other practical issues. Finding ingredients for daily meals, ensuring that someone is working at the reception desk, running the café, managing the hotel spaces where individuals or families are accommodated, bringing children to school, and many other tasks require time and labor management by both refugees and locals.

This circumstance removes the duality of host and guest and allows us to understand the specificity of the City Plaza not simply as a place of refugee hosting or shelter but as a place where shared vulnerabilities and precariousness in the face of the ongoing urban economic and refugee crises create the commons. In a sense this process has engendered a new community that re-forms itself over time through the struggle with the design and condition of the hotel building. City Plaza reports that, funded only by small donations and fund-raising efforts by ordinary people, it has hosted around fifteen hundred people, enrolled eighty children in school, and provided residents with three meals daily and all hygiene necessities and medical care.[9] It has also managed to make this place a hub of solidarity, self-organization, and humanity.

The hotel was closed for seven years before its occupation. An open letter that the activists, calling themselves Refugee Accommodation Space

10.
Ibid.
11.
Vicki Squire, "Mobile
Solidarities and Precari-
ousness at City Plaza:
Beyond Vulnerable and
Disposable Lives," *Studies
in Social Justice* 12, no. 1
(2018): 124.
12.
Raj Patel, "The Hungry
of the Earth," *Radical
Philosophy*, no. 151
(2008), www
.radicalphilosophyarchive
.com/wp-content
/files_mf/rp151
_commentary
_hungryoftheearth
_patel.pdf.
13.
See Stavrides, *Common
Space*.

City Plaza, wrote to the owner of the hotel was prompted by a dispute over a water bill. The letter begins by discussing the circumstances surrounding the bankruptcy of the hotel. A court granted former employees of the hotel ownership of the furniture and other movable equipment in the building as compensation for unpaid wages, but the owner allegedly did not allow the workers to recover this property. When the building began to house refugees, the former employees granted permission for the use of the equipment by the residents. The letter also reveals the research that the activists conducted into the owner and her family: "Through no fault of your own, of course, your father, Evgenios, as a high ranking official at the Ministry of Industry, made use of his links to well known figures in the 'Nation-Saving revolution' of 21st April 1967 (the 1967–1974 junta regime), so as to undertake extremely profitable construction activities which, inevitably, also secured your own future. City Plaza is but one element of that, which was constructed during that period and which is full of construction code violations."[10]

I see the letter not only as a manifesto of City Plaza, giving information about the history of the hotel, but also as cross-cutting realities of past political, economic, and housing crises in Greece that are echoed in the current refugee housing crisis. As the researcher Vicki Squire has observed: "What is significant here is that the open letter highlights both aspects of precarity that are shared, as well as inequalities that emerge through the uneven experience of precariousness. For example, while there are particular barriers for new arrivals to secure labour opportunities, there are also difficulties in this regard for host populations as well . . . . Yet the emphasis on the wealth of some coming at the expense of others also highlights a wider sense of precarity as shared."[11]

The food activist Raj Patel has looked at the part that food has played in social movements—for example, the Black Panthers' free breakfast program for schoolchildren; the People's Grocery in Oakland; or Via Campesina, the international peasants' movement—helping to create different forms of solidarity. According to his definition, "Commons is about how we manage resources together."[12] But his argument is not only about managing and sustaining the cultivation and sharing of food but also about how food-related movements should act in solidarity with other movements. Thus the concept of "commons," as understood here, holds a sensitive position within any given community or public, especially in contested territories or cities subject to the threat of neoliberal destruction of the built environment. Negotiation and the resolution of conflicting values are key to such commoning practices. As Stavrides argues, more than the act or fact of sharing, it is the existence of common grounds for negotiation that is most important.[13]

City Plaza is near Victoria Square, where many solidarity groups are active and many types of migrants mingle, sharing the public space during the day. But this part of the city is also known

Fig. 3
Activist painting a poster in support of open borders in Europe.
Photo: City Plaza Collective

Fig. 4
Children playing at City Plaza hotel. Photo: City Plaza Collective

as the home of far-right fascist groups that threaten the migrants and activists. Olga Lafazani, a researcher and City Plaza member, explains that "the location of the building, in the Agios Panteleimonas area, was also a political decision. This Athens neighbourhood was where the far-right party 'Golden Dawn' first came together and holds a strong social base to this day. In such a neighbourhood, City Plaza forms a space of everyday encounter and intervention. It also exists as an organised space that acts as a barricade to fascist action." Conceptualizing commons with reference to the public does not focus so much on similarities or commonalities but on exploring the very differences between people on a purposefully instituted common ground, thus establishing grounds for negotiation rather than affirming that which is shared. Lafazani writes:

> What we proposed—namely, co-habitation in dignified conditions in the heart of the city—went against the social and spatial exclusion of the camps. It was also a counter-attack against the illegalization of the anti-racist movement by mustering an excess of solidarity and grassroots self-organisation. It organises everyday life while furthering the broader struggle for rights and freedom. Day to day, City Plaza proves that if the antagonistic social movement—with access to limited resources; without any institutional or organisational funding; reliant only on donations; without

14.
Olga Lafazani, "1.5 Year City Plaza: A Project on the Antipodes of Bordering and Control Policies," Antipode Foundation, November 13, 2017, wp.me/p16RPC-1FO.

15.
J. K. Gibson-Graham, "Introduction to the New Edition: Ten Years On," in *The End of Capitalism (as We Knew It): A Feminist Critique of Political Economy* (Minneapolis: University of Minnesota Press, 2006), xvii.

employees and "specialists"—can run one of the best spaces for housing refugees in Greece, then the model of the "camp" becomes a question of political choice. Through the counter-example of City Plaza, we challenge the dominant narrative that "there is no alternative" to camps, within the discourse of the "emergency" and "refugee crisis."[14]

In conclusion, commoning practices require creating models of criticality that are connected to new forms of communality through places, infrastructures, and buildings. Commoning practices enforce "collective" effort (collective action) and forms of cohabitation and collective precariousness. According to J. K. Gibson-Graham, "The 'collective' in this context does not suggest the massing together of like subjects, nor should the term

'action' imply an efficacy that originates in intentional beings or that is distinct from thought. We are trying for a broad and distributed notion of collective action, in order to recognize and keep open possibilities of connection and development."[15] Collective action requires the ethics of a community economy. Self-organization is not a simple hierarchy based on certain labor activities and their division but, conversely, a work/labor structure that allows activists and refugees to engage in different kinds of labor and share tasks. To reiterate Stavrides's analysis, collaboration is not about affirmation but about negotiation. City Plaza as a space of a commoning practices among activists, citizens, and refugees presents a solidarity infrastructure based on shared vulnerabilities at a small scale, one that may serve as a model.

Dearborn Park, looking north from Washington Street, ca. 1890. Courtesy Chicago Public Library Special Collections

Dearborn Park became a park almost as an afterthought. Located on land left over from a former military encampment, the park got its name from the recently decommissioned Fort Dearborn. By the mid-nineteenth century Dearborn Park's lakefront location was surrounded on three sides by industry and warehouses. It became a place of organized labor rallies and political speeches; attempts to landscape the grounds were often thwarted when plants were trampled during spirited public gatherings. Following the US Civil War of the 1860s, proposals were made to dedicate Dearborn Park as a place of memory and a memorial to the war dead. A gathering place and museum were planned for the site. Instead, the entire block was covered with a monumental Beaux-Arts structure built to house the first permanent home of the Chicago Public Library, marking the final years for Dearborn Park. Completed in 1897, the building incorporated the proposed war memorial in the Grand Army of the Republic Memorial Hall and maintained its identity as a place of open public gathering, often referred to as the People's Palace. By the 1970s the library had outgrown the building, which underwent a gradual conversion into today's Chicago Cultural Center, a public forum for cultural activities and the "living room of the city."
    —Tim Samuelson

Fight school segregation!

LET CHICAGO KNOW YOU WANT EQUAL EDUCATION FOR YOUR CHILDREN! HIT BACK AT CZAR BEN WILLIS AND HIS DOORMAT SCHOOL BOARD!

This is your chance to tell the world how you feel about the die-hard, obstructionist Public School officials who refuse to give ALL of Chicago's children an equal chance to get a good education.

Help put an end to inferior, overcrowded schooling! Help to end the ruinous segregation of our children! Help to rid Chicago of Ben Willis and the School Board members who have surrendered to him! Support this great protest — and get your friends to support it — RIGHT NOW!

KEEP YOUR CHILDREN OUT OF SCHOOL for this one day!

Let them know you want a better future for them

OCT. 22

FREEDOM DAY
SCHOOL BOYCOTT

Sponsored by Coordinating Council of Community Organizations

Gift: Catholic Interracial Council, 1/69
Cat. 10¼ x 8 in.
Education, Chicago.
[1963]

Flyer advertising the Freedom Day School Boycott to protest school segregation (recto and verso), 1963. Courtesy Chicago History Museum (ICHi-020839 and ICHi-020840)

On October 22, 1963, nearly 225,000 students stayed out of school for the citywide Freedom Day boycott. Downtown Chicago was filled with black students, parents, and supporters protesting racism in Chicago Public Schools (CPS). Organizers from the Coordinating Council of Community Organizations argued that CPS superintendent Benjamin Willis was maintaining a segregated, separate, and unequal school system. Black children attended schools that were under-resourced and underfunded, operating on double shifts to accommodate overcrowding. The school system installed mobile classrooms—dubbed Willis Wagons—to relieve overcrowding in black schools

WANTED—Thousands of Freedom Marchers

MEET at City Hall
(La Salle Street Side)

MARCH
to the Board of Education

SHOW CHICAGO YOU'RE SICK OF BEN WILLIS-ISM AND 2ND RATE EDUCATION—RIGHT NOW!

Freedom Day, OCTOBER 22, is the big day to let Mayor Daley know that it's his job to give Chicago a School Board which will truly serve ALL the people equally. So help to shout it loud and clear by coming to City Hall and marching with the thousands who demand ACTION NOW — for a better future for our children.

This is it! Will YOU be there?

Join the Freedom March on City Hall

TUES. OCT. 22 4 P.M.

You Can Help to do the job

Call your friends! Help spread the word about Freedom Day. Get the facts and leaflets for all — at Headquarters:

Appomatox Club
3632 S. Parkway
Phone: 285–1282

---

rather than allow black students access to open seats in white schools. At black neighborhood schools, demonstrators, often led by black women and parents, increasingly protested the installation of Willis Wagons. Freedom Day organizers built on the energy of these neighborhood-based protests. In addition to calling for desegregation, organizers put forth a vision of the equitable access to resources that they wanted and deserved. "Every child should have an equal opportunity to get a good education," the protesters insisted. Black children marched and chanted, "What do we want? Books! When? Now!" Not all their demands were met, but after a protracted struggle, Superintendent Willis stepped down.
    —Elizabeth Todd-Breland

NOURISHING THE ROOT: TRANSFORMING THE URBAN ECOLOGIES OF CHICAGO

SEPAKE ANGIAMA AND EMMANUEL PRATT

Emmanuel Pratt is the cofounder and executive director of Sweet Water Foundation, an emerging community land trust in the heart of Chicago's South Side. Sweet Water Foundation's practice of regenerative neighborhood development is a creative social justice method that produces safe and inspiring spaces and curates healthy intergenerational communities that transform the ecology of once- "blighted" neighborhoods. Here Pratt speaks about reclaiming space and language, restituting and regenerating the land through skill sharing, and recognizing the need to collectively nourish the root as an act of radical awakening.

SEPAKE ANGIAMA: There are two things you've said about how language is appropriated and used in different ways that really struck me. The first has to do with the term *blight* and specifically *urban blight*. The second is the question of what *radical* means and its etymology. In your practice you relate both terms to the land.

EMMANUEL PRATT: So the term *blight* is actually borrowed from agriculture, referring to the death and decay of a crop so that it no longer sustains life. As cities began to evolve in the twentieth century, the term *blight* began to be used in reference to the process of economic devaluation and degradation of a property or neighborhood. If I'm not mistaken, Lewis Mumford was first recognized for using *blight* in reference to the process of urban decay. Others followed, using the term as a framework for understanding land economics, particularly during the rise of slums and the housing crisis during the Great Depression but more specifically with the influx of African Americans into northern cities during the Great Migration. African American neighborhoods in cities like Chicago were consistently identified as "blighted"—written off as spaces of concentrated poverty, plagued by decay, and ultimately in need of erasure and redevelopment. As urban renewal policies increasingly targeted these "blighted" neighborhoods, the practice of urban renewal very quickly and rightfully got the nickname "Negro removal" and ultimately gave rise to the nationwide practice of redlining.

So in every way our work at Sweet Water is a direct response to the ecology of absence that has been constructed from the application of this term *blight* to our neighborhoods and communities. Our work flips the concept of blight on its head by celebrating the abundance of life that exists in these same so-called blighted neighborhoods.

Over the past five years the team at Sweet Water Foundation has transformed four contiguous city blocks of empty spaces on the South Side into a place now known as the Perry Ave Commons. The work includes approximately three acres of urban farms and a large community garden, one formerly foreclosed home transformed into a community school space [Think-Do House], another abandoned home currently being transformed into a live-work space for apprentices and international networks of artists/designers [Reconstruction House], a greenhouse converted into a community-based woodshop and classroom space [Work-Shop], a shipping container converted into a learning laboratory and greenhouse [Think-Do Pod], and at the center of the Commons, situated directly on the Perry Ave Community Farm, is a large-scale, timber-frame mortise-and-tenon pavilion that serves as a central space for large community gatherings, cultural celebrations, and performing arts [Thought Barn].

From *blight* to *light* .... This place has its own body of language celebrating the process of reconstruction and healing. Everything echoes the possibility of hope. There *grows* the neighborhood—calling into question the age-old saying "There goes the neighborhood."

SA   So part of what you're doing is building better context for language. Can you also talk about the word *radical*?

EP   Most people associate the term *radical* with extreme or terror—particularly in this political climate. We have to remind people that the actual definition of *radical* means "of or restoring to the root."

SA   Right. So do you relate to your practice as radical?

EP   Very much so. The work of transforming empty spaces into a *place* over a period of time is ultimately about celebrating the active and emergent process of rerooting. The Perry Ave Commons is in an area that was directly impacted by the process of redlining. Most members of the community that we serve consistently face the prospect of being displaced and uprooted—through eviction, gentrification, slumlording, school closures, incarceration, and so on. Traditional capital flows are extremely limited within this neighborhood.

So instead of following conventional development patterns founded on single bottom-line returns on investment, the Perry Ave Commons offers an example of a regenerative and adaptive framework that maximizes the assets and skill sets that exist within the community. But that requires a localized understanding of how people are employed, an understanding of the complexities and context that they're dealing with and the in-between moments of informality, those interstitial spaces that renegotiate the connection back to the land and remaining rooted in place. Gardening and farming help literally and metaphorically to transform emptiness and voids into an active healing process responding to decades and generations of trauma. And as the aesthetics and the forms of the spaces and built environment evolve, so do the language and image of the place.

All of this requires a radical imagination.

SA   This in-betweenness—the interstitial spaces where you find this informality—reminds me of something Jane Jacobs wrote about. She said that informal structures, although they might look like chaos or mess, have their own logic. So it's quite interesting how you relate the logic of the local to planning systems. That's also the case in Johannesburg. Architects try to plan informal structures. For example, they think about how buses come in and out of certain localities to take people from place to place. How do you plan for something like a market, which already has its own logic and its own way of doing things, and how does that fit into a more formalized structure?

EP   Exactly. My favorite chapter from Jacobs's book *The Death and Life of Great American Cities* [1961] is the final chapter. Perhaps it's the most overlooked chapter as well: "The Kind of Problem a City Is." Ultimately there's a localized familiarity of day-to-day operations, and you constantly have to translate, iterate, and introduce something new and allow space and time for feedback—

SA   Right. It's a problem of not having that localized knowledge about space, time, and environmental conditions. So how do you think Sweet Water Foundation adapts to that way of thinking, which is much more about being responsive to place and people?

EP   A place truly becomes a place only by allowing for a frequency of iterative and localized responses.

For example, gardening and farming offer initial ways to begin to bring people together to share stories, to work, to feed, to heal, to find out about family histories, medical conditions, and the real value of food to a community. But when real, value-based transactions happen, real-world market relationships are formed, bonds are formed, and then bonds of trust are created. It is within the spaces of trust that place can be built.

SA   So this wasn't necessarily a means of commodifying the land but was much more about a co-social transaction that was taking place.

EP   It's about the reconnection.

SA   Yes, but you also used the word *translation*. Could you explain what you mean by that?

EP   There's a lived reality of existing in an area that doesn't have access to food, that doesn't have access to stable housing, doesn't have access to jobs. There are terms like *food desert* that are used externally. They're used in political jargon and in policy documents. But when you actually come to that site, there's an interesting gap between external perception and people who have been living like this for so long. It's just like the dated term *inner city*. It's been dated for decades, but it's still used—sometimes in order to say, "Well we've got to return some of these amenities back to these neighborhoods."
      Once it becomes recognized through research documents and money is poured in to study that situation, a term is codified. The terms then get placed into policy and popularized by mass media. Then the term gets introduced back into that neighborhood, and now everybody is talking about food deserts, but initially nobody was talking about food deserts, not locally.

SA   It comes back to language.

EP   It always comes back to language. This is critically important in my experience with architecture and the field of architecture; language is a way to create or crystallize a bond and trust with people, or it is used very divisively to alienate and can foster mistrust. Starting a conversation by saying, "Look, we want to put a garden into these lots," is very different from saying, "I want to juxtapose the dynamics of the modular designed object with these interstitial third spaces." People just don't know what you're talking about.

SA   Do you think it creates a kind of cognitive dissonance?

EP   Absolutely. And it creates a certain barrier to shared knowledge and understanding. When you put down a garden bed, that's cool, but if you put in a garden bed with this shape of a house on top of it, it becomes a sculptural object. It calls into question the idea of putting only a garden there. Why don't you just put something there as a marker at the threshold of the neighborhood? We hand-raised a barn in the neighborhood [Thought Barn] in 2017 because so many people were coming and we felt that we needed a centralized gathering place and a public space for performances.

SA   So the design followed a need?

EP   Yeah, absolutely. But it also raises questions: like why is there a barn in the city now? Why is there a farm in the city? How often are there farms in the city? And then it goes back to the reality that there was once a fire, the great fire of 1871 in Chicago. There was a moment when people were like, "Oh, no more barns within city limits," because they were fire hazards. When we first said we were designing a barn, everybody asked, "Where are the farm animals? Where are the tractors?" We were like, "No, it's actually for people." They were like, "Well, what does that mean?" Come and join us for an event and meet other people. People suggested that it shouldn't be enclosed and should just stay open-air, so that people passing by could see what's going on and be engaged.

This structure is also a great way to talk about other cultures, other traditions. Going to the Greco-Roman and the Egyptian ways of building, where you have multiple people and hands carrying a thousand pounds and of course Amish barn raising. It's very much a dialogic approach, not a monolithic one.

SA   Then you talk about a vision. Is it a collective or a shared vision? Where does that come from?

EP   That's a very complicated question. I go back to Jane Jacobs and her last chapter on what kinds of problems cities are. She said we've got it wrong in diagnosing cities using one formulaic approach.

SA   Sure.

EP   We need another approach. So ours, which people initially said was crazy, is more of a call-and-response framework. It's historically black, like in church. You put something out there, and you leave a space for somebody to respond.

It's like the marches in Johannesburg—when the ANC [African National Congress] was preparing and then marching through the streets. There's a very distinct call-and-response, which activates collectivity. It's like, "Are you really ready for this? Let's be ready."

SA   Right.

EP   There's a joy and celebration of possibility. There's this crazy moment of hope where there might typically be lots of doubt, despair, concern. Trajectories of history have said, "No, it's not possible." And we're saying, "It is possible. Let's go!" Yeah, it's black.

SA   To return to this notion of the "we," who does that "we" constitute for you?

EP   The "we" constitutes the Sweet Water core team.

SA   Who's that?

EP   There are gardeners, farmers, carpenters, mentors, apprentices. It's very intergenerational. We have a group of elders in their fifties and older who have lived life in every way, shape, and form and are looking at this as a possibility for the future and for their legacy. They want to give back; they want to build up. Then they find themselves reflected in a lot of our youth.

We've also begun to introduce new partners who have helped build up the place, leading tours, sharing their language, sharing their stories, and bonding with people from outside. Then there's some space for respect for what has been built in the "blight," you know? Sure, we'll use that term, but it's not going to define who we are. So then all of a sudden the "we" might include a university student studying public policy. Four years later we have fellows. They come in fellowship. So the "we" is this kind of emergent "we."

SA   Does it involve nonhumans?

EP   Of course. The "we" is first and foremost formed by the regenerative aspects of our plants. Why do we refer to this place as an urban ecology? Because it is a way to think about us living symbiotically with the land. And serving one another and the land. Building up new objects or a new home that was revitalized from this old home from 1891. It's right across the street from the farm and right next to the garden, with lines of sight, just as Jane Jacobs described. You can experience the community as it emerges. We're designing new housing from the ground up that embeds the labor, the practice, the modularity, the ecological responsibility, all that—and it introduces a new way of thinking about capital. It would be enticing for someone buying a home, who can afford to celebrate their privilege, to come in and bond with the person next door who built this place in the noosphere— the collective space of human thought.

Some of the "we" are the people who died. We forget, and some of the "we" are the memories (photos, diaries, journals) that we're finding in this house and piecing together. The people who lived here are informing how we're now reconstructing the space.

SA   That's really beautiful.

This conversation was recorded in Chicago on March 14, 2019.

THE HAYMARKET MEETING.—"In the Name of the People, I Command You to Disperse."

Above and opposite: Illustrations of the Haymarket Meeting and the Haymarket Riot, Chicago, from Michael J. Schaack, *Anarchy and Anarchists*, 1889. Courtesy Illinois History and Lincoln Collection, University of Illinois at Urbana-Champaign Library

People and persons. Two idioms. Providing people with security and welfare is a foundational conceit of the modern republic (*res publica*: the common thing). It gives meaning to the idea of political accountability, but it is not the terrain of responsibility. To be responsive to the ethical, political, and aesthetic demands of a moment is perhaps the defining quality of a person. Different persons respond differently, but respond we must. In May 1886 workers across Chicago demanded an eight-hour day. Only a government acting in the name of a people could guarantee such working conditions.

THE HAYMARKET RIOT. THE EXPLOSION AND THE CONFLICT.

The police ordered the workers to disperse in the name of the people. Someone hurled a bomb. The police opened fire, surrendering all personal qualities. Although the bomb thrower's identity was never discovered, seven workers were sentenced to death. The British Arts and Crafts theorist William Morris described their persecution as a menace to the liberal ideals of the American republic. Law cannot guarantee the common good, but it is right to want good laws. This is a quotidian desire. Ordinary. Commonplace. Demanding. It necessitates spaces where a person can reflect on their habits of response without remorse or recrimination. Where we can see ourselves and the world as others might.
—Shiben Banerji

CONCRETE
WINDOWS

STEPHEN
WILLATS

Living within the confines of my new home.

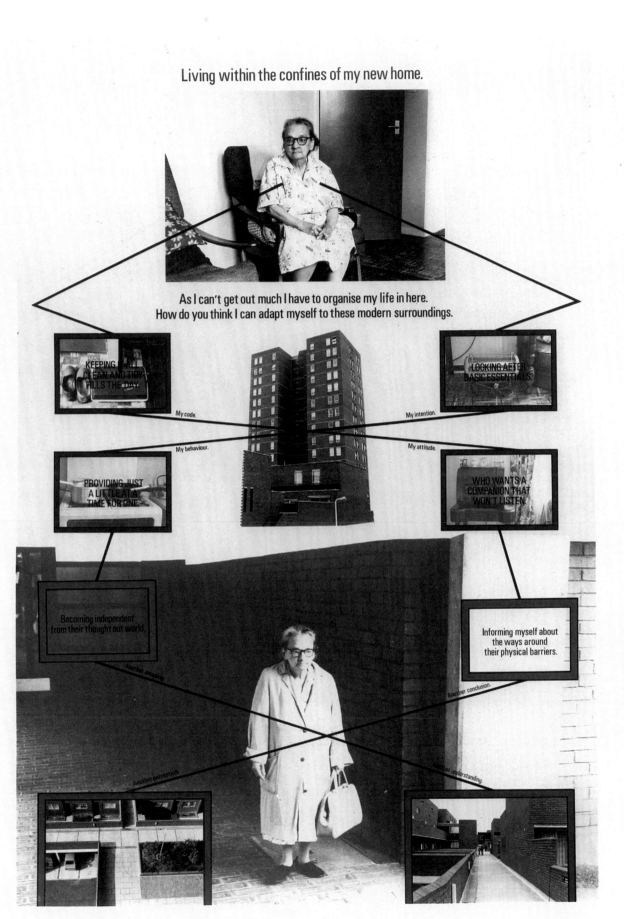

As I can't get out much I have to organise my life in here.
How do you think I can adapt myself to these modern surroundings.

KEEPING IT ALL CLEAN AND TIDY FILLS THE DAY.

LOOKING AFTER BASIC ESSENTIALS.

My code.

My intention.

My behaviour.

My attitude.

PROVIDING JUST A LITTLE AT A TIME FOR ONE.

WHO WANTS A COMPANION THAT WON'T LISTEN

Becoming independent from their thought out world.

Informing myself about the ways around their physical barriers.

Another meaning.

Another conclusion.

Another perception.

Another understanding.

Living with the present day limitations of a small income.

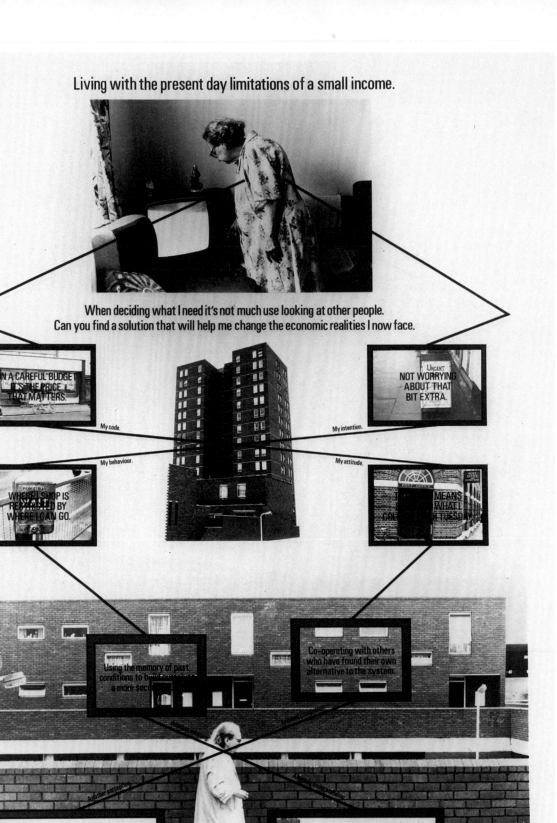

When deciding what I need it's not much use looking at other people.
Can you find a solution that will help me change the economic realities I now face.

ON A CAREFUL BUDGET IT'S THE PRICE THAT MATTERS.

NOT WORRYING ABOUT THAT BIT EXTRA.

My code.

My intention.

My behaviour.

My attitude.

WHERE I SHOP IS RESTRICTED BY WHERE I CAN GO.

MEANS WHAT I

Using the memory of past conditions to build ourselves a more secure

Co-operating with others who have found their own alternative to the system.

Another perception.

Living without the certainty that I will see someone tomorrow.

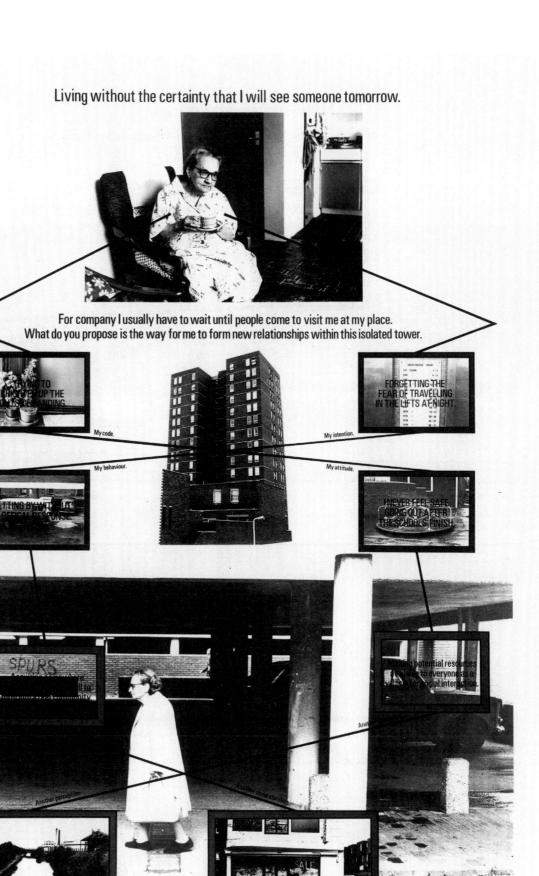

For company I usually have to wait until people come to visit me at my place.
What do you propose is the way for me to form new relationships within this isolated tower.

My code.

My intention.

My behaviour.

My attitude.

FORGETTING THE
FEAR OF TRAVELLING
IN THE LIFTS AT NIGHT.

I NEVER FEEL SAFE
GOING OUT AFTER
THE SCHOOLS FINISH

SPURS

Another perception.

Another understanding.

Trying to get on with my own way of life.

How can I maintain my real values within such regular surroundings.

It's what you make of yourself that counts.

Searching for domestic harmony within contained conditions.

How can we enjoy our privacy while extending life at home.

I DON'T LIKE A BARE ROOM

THERE'S NO SPACE FOR DRYING

WE HAVE TO SHOP IN TOWN FOR EVERYTHING

IT'S LOT'S WORSE WITH CHILDREN

Plan alterations together for the situation in which you will spend most time.

Striving all our working life against economic forces.

How can we afford the environment we would like for our family.

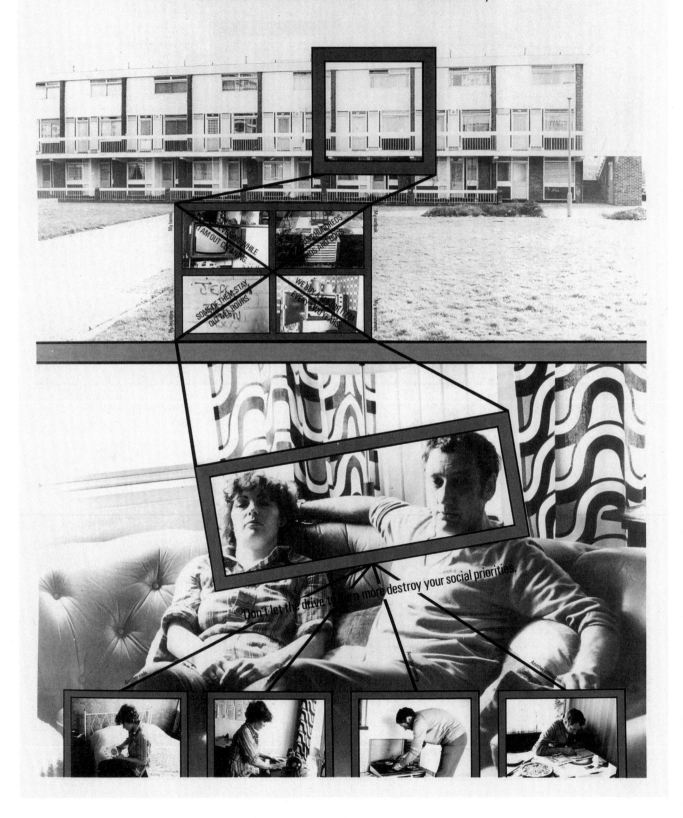

Don't let the drive to earn more destroy your social priorities.

Attempting to establish our own cultural life.

How can I find a way of expressing myself with my neighbours.

You don't know how many people would like to become involved until you ask.

YOU FEEL VERY CONDENSING
IT FEELS LIKE CONDENSING

I DO FEEL FREE IF I CAN PLAY IT AT VOLUME
THAT'S LIKE AN ENERGY TABLET FOR ME

NOW I SPEND MY WHOLE DAY INSIDE HERE
I HAD TO LEARN MY HOME ALL OVER AGAIN

ALTHOUGH I AM SITTING IN THIS ROOM
SOMETIMES I FEEL AS IF I AM IN TRINIDAD

Pages 157–59
Living with Practical Realities, 1978. Photographic paper prints, ink, and Letraset text on board; three panels, each 30 × 42 ⅞ in. (76 × 109 cm). Tate Gallery, London

Pages 160–63
Learning to Live within a Confined Space, 1978. Photographic paper prints, gouache, ink, and Letraset text on board; four panels, each 39 ⅜ × 52 in. (100 × 132 cm). Migros Museum, Zurich

Pages 164–66
A View Over the Balcony, 1991. Photographic paper prints, photographic dye, acrylic paint, and Letraset text on board; three panels, each 30 ⁵⁄₁₆ × 50 in. (77 × 127 cm). Private collection

FEATURED BIENNIAL CONTRIBUTORS

FOR A COMPLETE LIST OF BIENNIAL CONTRIBUTORS AS OF JULY 12, 2019,
SEE PP. 212–13. PUBLICATION CONTRIBUTORS ARE REPRESENTED ON PP. 202–6.

AKINBODE AKINBIYI
Born 1946, Oxford, England;
lives and works in Berlin

Initially rooted in the fields of architecture and journalism, the photographer Akinbode Akinbiyi struck out on the proverbial artist's path with a focus on sprawling megacities, especially those on the African continent. He wandered the highways and byways of places like Addis Ababa, Cairo, Johannesburg, Kano, and Lagos, searching for moments of pure serendipity. In 2017 he was invited to *Documenta 14*, which prompted him to move toward a broader narrative, expressed in the title of the images presented there: *Passageways, Involuntary Narratives, and the Sound of Crowded Spaces*. These images came from urban locations as disparate as Athens, Berlin, Lagos, and Philadelphia, and they sought to uncover the spiritual undercurrents that define our everyday meanderings. Today, Akinbiyi continues to document major cities as well as smaller locales, including Bamako, Mali; Cotonou, Benin; Dakar, Senegal; Durban, South Africa; Ibadan, Nigeria; Khartoum, Sudan; Lubumbashi, Democratic Republic of the Congo; and Maputo, Mozambique.

Berlin-Moabit, Berlin, 2016. Inkjet print, 23 ⅝ × 23 ⅝ in. (60 × 60 cm)

ARCHITECTURE FOR ALL
(HERKES İÇIN MIMARLIK)
Established 2011, Istanbul

Committed to finding creative ways to address social problems, Architecture for All initiates design and architecture projects in communities throughout Turkey. The organization has hosted planning workshops, temporary events, and design-build projects that aim to improve the social, environmental, and economic conditions of the built environment. Its projects are facilitated by multidisciplinary teams equipped to respond to complex public needs. One of its earliest projects aimed to create tools and prototypes for retrofitting thousands of vacant schools in rural Turkey that were abandoned due to changes in the educational system. Since 2011 members and volunteers have facilitated participatory workshops focusing on renovation of the school buildings as well as ideas about rural life and economic opportunity. The organization's work has been exhibited and collected internationally, including at the Victoria and Albert Museum, London; the Venice Biennale of Architecture; the Art Institute of Chicago; MAXXI, Rome; and the Istanbul Design Biennial.

Yırca Soaphouse Project construction workshop, Soma, Turkey, 2017. Photo: Herkes İçin Mimarlık Association

SAMMY BALOJI AND FILIP DE BOECK
Born 1978, Lubumbashi, Democratic
Republic of the Congo
Born 1961, Antwerp, Belgium
Both live and work between Brussels and
the Democratic Republic of the Congo

Sammy Baloji mines the archive, traces social history in architecture and landscape, and probes the body as a site of memory and witness to operations of power in order to create photography and multimedia installations that expose tensions past and present. Filip De Boeck is a writer, filmmaker, curator, and professor of anthropology at the University of Leuven whose research focuses on youth and the politics of culture, urban infrastructure, and the transformation of private and public space in urban Africa. In 2016 the pair collaborated to create the exhibition *Urban Now: City Life in Congo* and the accompanying publication *Suturing the City: Living Together in Congo's Urban Worlds*—endeavors that underscored the intersection of contemporary art and anthropology. Building on the success of their earlier collaboration, they are currently at work on a new project about colonial and postcolonial migration across the Congolese-Angolan border and the impact of migration on Congo's sociopolitical history.

Sammy Baloji, *Cielux OCPT building exterior, municipality of Masina*, 2013, from the series *Urban Now: City Life in Congo*, 2016. Inkjet print, 39 ⅜ × 59 in. (100 × 150 cm)

BLACK QUANTUM FUTURISM
Established 2015, Philadelphia

Black Quantum Futurism (BQF), the interdisciplinary creative practice of Camae Ayewa and Rasheedah Phillips, weaves quantum physics, Afrofuturism, and Afrodiasporic concepts of time, ritual, text, and sound to present innovative tools for escaping negative temporal loops, oppression vortexes, and the digital matrix. BQF has created a number of community-based projects, performances, experimental music projects, installations, workshops, books, short films, and zines, including the award-winning Community Futures Lab. BQF is a Velocity Fund grantee (2018), a Solitude × ZKM web resident (2018), a Center for Emerging Visual Artists Fellow (2017), a Pew Fellow (2017), a Blade of Grass Fellow (2016), and an artist-in-residence at West Philadelphia Neighborhood Time Exchange (2015). BQF has presented, exhibited, and performed at such venues as Red Bull Arts, New York; Serpentine Gallery, London; Philadelphia Museum of Art; Open Engagement at MoMA PS1, Long Island City, New York; Bergen Kunsthall, Norway; Le Gaîté Lyrique, Paris; and Squeaky Wheel Film & Media Art Center, Buffalo.

Alter-Native Time Portal, 2017. Installation view at the Perelman Building, Philadelphia Museum of Art, 2018

ADRIAN BLACKWELL
Born 1966, Toronto; lives and works in Toronto

Spanning photography, video, sculpture, urban theory, and design, Adrian Blackwell's practice responds to the political and economic forces inscribed in physical spaces. His work often consists of interventions that directly address pressing urban issues, exposing the powers and interests that shape the city. His projects unfold in conjunction with research focused on the local and global effects of neoliberal urbanization, the disappearance of public and affordable housing in North America, and the inherent paradoxes of urban space. Blackwell's work has been exhibited at artist-run centers and public institutions across Canada, at the 2005 Shenzhen Biennale, the 2011 Chengdu Biennale, and the Architectural Association, London. He will participate in the inaugural 2019 Toronto Biennial of Art. He has taught architecture and urbanism at Chongqing University (China), the University of Michigan, Harvard University, and the University of Toronto, and he is currently an assistant professor at the University of Waterloo (Canada).

Model for a Public Space (knot), 2010. Installation view at Justina M. Barnicke Gallery, University of Toronto Art Centre, 2010. Photo: Jesse Colin Jackson

BORDERLESS STUDIO
Established 2016, Chicago

Founded by architect, urban designer, and educator Paola Aguirre Serrano, the Chicago-based collaborative research and design practice Borderless Studio takes a holistic approach to complex city systems, emphasizing civic engagement and interdisciplinary collaboration as fundamental elements of equitable community design processes. Conceived as a combination design studio and workshop, Borderless often finds itself at the center of collaborative, community-based projects, addressing issues of social equity, shared resources, and neighborhood development. It invests heavily in research and education, drawing expertise from the arenas of architecture, landscape design, community activism, and public service to shape processes and plans that are inclusive of diverse stakeholders. Aguirre Serrano is widely recognized for her leadership in multidisciplinary urban design, contributing regularly to published writings on the subject, organizing workshops, and teaching at institutions such as the School of the Art Institute of Chicago. Her honors include being named to Next City Vanguard's (2016) and Impact Design Hub's (2017) 40 Under 40 lists and receiving the American Planning Association–Illinois Chapter Emerging Planner Award (2018).

Chicago Extra-Large–Closed Public Schools, 2017–18. Map installation at the now-closed Anthony Overton Elementary School, Chicago

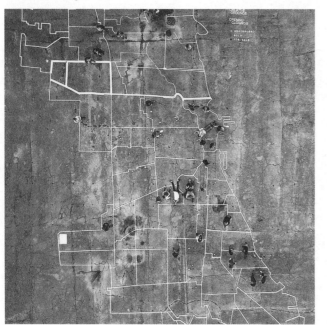

TANIA BRUGUERA AND ASOCIACIÓN DE ARTE ÚTIL
Born 1968, Havana;
lives and works in New York
Established 2011, New York;
Eindhoven, the Netherlands;
and Coniston, England

For more than twenty-five years, Tania Bruguera has created socially engaged performances and installations that examine the nature of political power structures and their effect on the lives of constituents. Her works often expose the social effects of political forces and present global issues of power, migration, censorship, and repression through participatory projects that turn viewers into "citizens." Bruguera is a recipient of the School of the Art Institute of Chicago's Honoris Causa and was named one of the Hundred Leading Global Thinkers by *Foreign Policy* magazine. She recently opened the Hannah Arendt International Institute for Artivism in Havana—a school, exhibition space, and think tank enabling collaboration between activist artists and everyday Cubans. In collaboration with museums and art institutions worldwide, Bruguera initiated the Asociación de Arte Útil, an international network that promotes the usefulness of art and its integration into everyday life through research, workshops, and other programs.

Escuela de Arte Útil, Yerba Buena Center for the Arts, San Francisco, 2017

CAMP
Established 2007, Mumbai

Based in Chuim village, Mumbai, CAMP is not an artists' collective but rather a studio in which ideas and energies gather and become interests and forms. Its members—a group of artists, filmmakers, software programmers, architects, activists, archivists, and autonomous researchers—produce works of video, film, and electronic media, as well as a variety of public art projects. In addition, they run the online video archives Pad.ma and Indiancine.ma as well as R and R, a community cultural space in the Mumbai suburb of Mankhurd. They are also noted for their film screening series Evenings at CAMP Rooftop. CAMP's work has appeared at venues throughout the world, including at the Museum of Modern Art in New York, *documenta 13*, Tate Modern, and the Gwangju, Taipei, Shanghai, Sharjah, and Kochi-Muziris biennials. In 2015, the group presented *As If I-V*, a major survey of its work across five solo exhibitions in Kolkata, New Delhi, and Mumbai.

Rendering of *Matrix*, 2017. Installation at Theater Münster, Germany

CAROLINA CAYCEDO
Born 1978, London;
lives and works in Los Angeles

Carolina Caycedo participates in movements of territorial resistance, solidarity economies, and housing as a human right. Her artistic practice includes a collective dimension, in which performances, drawings, photographs, and videos are not just end results but integral parts of her process. Her work contributes to the construction of environmental historical memory as a fundamental element for nonrepetition of violence against human and nonhuman entities, generating debate about the future in relation to common goods, environmental justice, just energy transition, and cultural biodiversity. Caycedo's work will be featured in upcoming solo exhibitions at Muzeum Sztuki, Łódź, Poland; Orange County Museum of Art, Santa Ana, California; and the Institute of Contemporary Art Boston. She is a 2019 participant in the 45 Salón Nacional de Artistas in Colombia and Art Basel in Switzerland, and she will be a 2020 visiting artist at the NTU Centre for Contemporary Art in Singapore.

Yuma, or the Land of Friends, 2017. Installation view at *Berlin Biennale 8*

ALEJANDRA CELEDÓN AND NICOLÁS STUTZIN
Born 1979, Edmonton, Canada;
lives and works in Santiago, Chile
Born 1981, Santiago, Chile;
lives and works in Santiago

Alejandra Celedón and Nicolás Stutzin are architects and scholars who engage architectural history and the use of public space. When Celedón curated the Chilean Pavilion at the Venice Architecture Biennale in 2018, she conceived an architectural, graphic, and artistic response to the biennale's theme of "Freespace," creating a critical reconstruction of the floor of the National Stadium in Santiago that represented the city. Celedón is a professor at the Pontificia Universidad Católica de Chile and holds a PhD in the history and theory of architecture from the Architectural Association School of Architecture. Her curating partner, Nicolás Stutzin, is an associate professor at the School of Architecture, Universidad Diego Portales, and adjunct assistant professor at the School of Architecture, Pontificia Universidad Católica de Chile, who engages with architectural theory, public architecture, and urban planning. Since 2006 Stutzin has worked independently as an architect in a wide range of scales. He holds a master of science degree in advanced architectural design from Columbia University.

Alejandra Celedón, *Stadium* for the Chilean Pavilion at the Venice Architecture Biennale, 2018

CENTER FOR SPATIAL RESEARCH
Established 2015, New York

The Center for Spatial Research (CSR) at Columbia University focuses on spatial data analysis at the intersection of design, architecture, urbanism, the humanities, and data science. CSR engages with data in order to understand the forces transforming cities today and to investigate the effects that data-based approaches to urban studies have on cities themselves. Its projects involve collaborations with researchers and advocates across disciplines and institutions. Recent CSR exhibitions include In Plain Sight at the 2018 Venice Biennale of Architecture; *Conflict Urbanism: Aleppo* at the 2016 Istanbul Design Biennial; and *The Brain Index*, an installation at the Zuckerman Institute on Columbia's Manhattanville campus. CSR was founded through a grant from the Andrew W. Mellon Foundation and has received support from the Ford Foundation and the David Lion Gardiner Foundation. It builds on the work of Columbia's Spatial Information Design Lab in the Graduate School of Architecture, Planning and Preservation.

Conflict Urbanism: Colombia, 2016–17

CHICAGO ARCHITECTURAL PRESERVATION ARCHIVE
Established 2018, Chicago

The Chicago Architectural Preservation Archive (CAPA) is devoted to the documentation and stewardship of materials related to the efforts of early urban preservationists. CAPA is led by director Tim Samuelson, an architectural historian and preservationist who has also served as cultural historian for the city of Chicago since 2002, and associate director Bianca Bova, a Chicago-based curator and art critic. Housed by Mana Contemporary Chicago, the archive's holdings include collections of architectural salvage, photography, research documents, and realia with ties to the First Chicago School of Architecture. The archive is accessible to independent scholars, artists, and interested members of the public. CAPA has cohosted public programming in collaboration with Chicago architecture group MAScontext; loaned material to other institutions for exhibition; and staged multiple exhibitions in Ludwig Mies van der Rohe's S. R. Crown Hall. Its preservation initiatives have included assisting with the archaeological excavation and assessment, in spring 2018, of remnants of the historic Mecca Flat apartments.

Floor tiles from the Mecca Flats unearthed for conservation, 2018

COHABITATION STRATEGIES AND URBAN FRONT
Established 2008, Rotterdam
Established 2019, New York

The brainchild of Lucia Babina, Emiliano Gandolfi, Gabriela Rendon, and Miguel Robles-Duran, Cohabitation Strategies (CohStra) emerged as a response to contemporary urban structures and neoliberal practices that its founders believed were propelling social inequities among citizens. The nonprofit cooperative—which launched the same day as the historic Lehman Brothers bank collapse—conducts sociospatial research and development around the world, formulating long-term strategies with the input of artistic, scientific, and community perspectives. Urban Front is a recently established international consultancy network for governments, NGOs, and foundations looking to mitigate social inequalities. An outgrowth of CohStra's work that expanded the organization's global capacity, it was founded by Robles-Duran and David Harvey, who are recognized as leading scholars of urbanism and urban geography as well as outspoken proponents of the modern "right to the city" movement. CohStra's community-driven projects have been featured at the Museum of Modern Art, the Venice Biennale of Architecture, the Istanbul Design Biennial, and the Shenzhen Biennale.

Playgrounds for Useful Knowledge, Action 1: Sharing Knowledge, Philadelphia, 2015

CONSTRUCTLAB
Established 1995, Berlin

ConstructLab takes a dynamic approach to uniting architectural concept and construction. Breaking with traditional divisions of labor, the organization engages a team of multitalented designer-builders—as well as sociologists, urban planners, graphic designers, curators, educators, and web developers—who carry the creative process from the drafting table into the field, enabling design to respond to the possibilities and restraints posed by materials, site, environment, and utilization. With emphasis on collaboration, both with one another and with members of the community, ConstructLab's practitioners take on a variety of projects, permanent and temporary, bringing their creative strategies to bear in solving problems and raising awareness of social, environmental, and practical issues. They favor recycled and upcycled materials, and they are mindful of resources available locally. At the heart of ConstructLab's work, which includes commissioned projects throughout Europe and in the United States, is a desire to enhance feelings of community and heighten the sense of place.

Poster for Mon(s) Invisible–Jardin Suspendu, part of Mons European Capital of Culture 2015

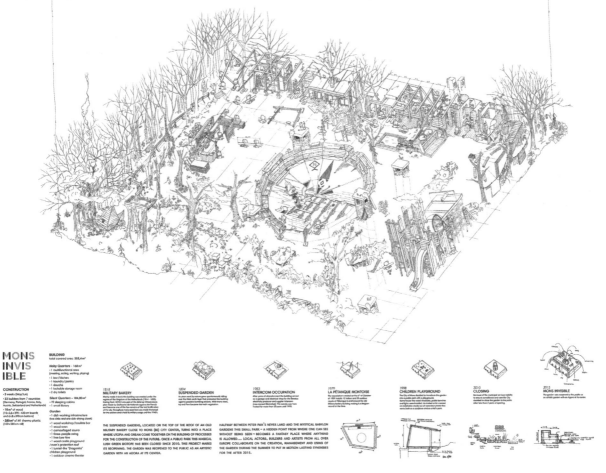

DAAR
(DECOLONIZING ARCHITECTURE
ART RESIDENCY)
Established 2007, Beit Sahour, Palestine
Alessandro Petti and Sandi Hilal with
Isshaq Al Barbary, Husam Abu Salem,
Elsa Koehler, and Sandy Rishmawi.
Photographic Dossier by Luca Capuano

DAAR (Decolonizing Architecture Art
Residency) was founded in 2007 with the aim
of gathering architects, artists, activists,
urbanists, filmmakers, and curators to work
collectively on issues of politics and architecture. Today, DAAR develops theoretically
ambitious and practically engaged research
projects related to the struggle for justice
and equality. Its latest publication, *Permanent
Temporariness* (2019), is a book, a catalogue,
and an archive that accounts for fifteen years
of research, experimentation, and creation
marked by an inner tension and a visionary
drive that rethinks itself through collective
engagement. DAAR has participated in the
Venice Biennale (2003, 2008, 2009, 2013, 2015),
the Istanbul Biennial (2009), Home Works
Beirut (2010), the Bienal de São Paulo (2014),
the Asian Art Biennial (2015), the Marrakesh
Biennial (2016), and Qalandiya International
(2016). Major retrospectives of their work
were inaugurated at New York University Abu
Dhabi Art Gallery (2018) and Van Abbemuseum,
Eindhoven, Netherlands (2019).

Installation view of *Refugee Heritage (part I)*, Van
Abbemuseum, Eindhoven, 2015

CITY OF DETROIT PLANNING AND DEVELOPMENT DEPARTMENT
Restructured 2016, Detroit

The City of Detroit Planning and Development Department (PDD) has the auspicious responsibility of governing sustainable development—including building preservation—in America's largest postindustrial city. The PDD is emboldened by the tenacity and resourcefulness of Detroit's citizenry, who have remained resilient and undeterred through long-term industrial decline, municipal disinvestment, and bankruptcy. Engaging fully with these residents, the PDD is creating a palimpsest of progressive strategies aimed at rebuilding a city "secure in its future, grounded in its roots, and hopeful in its present state." Key to this mission is the goal of engendering an atmosphere of trust by creating local opportunity, promoting equitable development without displacement, and supporting inclusionary growth. Moreover, the PDD seeks to advance design as a means of improving quality of life for all people, celebrating the city's design legacy, and contributing to its design future, all while balancing function with beauty.

FICA—FUNDO IMOBILIÁRIO COMUNITÁRIO PARA ALUGUEL
Established 2015, São Paulo

In 2015 a group of professionals and activists in São Paulo decided to take action to confront gentrification, segregation, and evictions in large Brazilian cities. The result was FICA, or Fundo Imobiliário Comunitário para Aluguel (Community Rental Real Estate Fund), a nonprofit organization that is pioneering the implementation of social ownership in Brazil. FICA works on three fronts: acquiring, refurbishing, and renting apartments to low-income families at accessible rates; promoting public policies that take into account community ownership and social rent; and developing events and research to debate and structure public action toward a more equal city. FICA has organized talks and seminars on alternative ownership and rental models and has promoted hands-on design and carpentry workshops for a wide audience, including students and residents of social housing. FICA raises funds through crowdfunding and is now working to expand its common-property model to encompass other uses, such as sustainable agriculture.

Workshop at Apartment 1, 2017. Installation view at the 11th São Paulo Architecture Biennial

Community engagement meeting for the Grand River–Northwest Neighborbood Framework Plan, Detroit, 2017

FORENSIC ARCHITECTURE AND INVISIBLE INSTITUTE
Established 2011, London
Established 2014, Chicago

Forensic Architecture is a research agency composed of architects, artists, scholars, filmmakers, lawyers, and scientists that develops spatial, architectural, media, and cartographic techniques to investigate human rights and environmental violations and support communities exposed to state violence and persecution. The resulting architectural evidence is presented in international courtrooms, parliamentary inquiries, United Nations assemblies, citizens' tribunals, and exhibitions and publications. Based at Goldsmiths, University of London, the agency has received commissions from organizations such as the New York Times, Praxis Films, BBC Africa Eye, Amnesty International, and the Bureau of Investigative Journalism. The Invisible Institute is a journalism production company based on Chicago's South Side that is guided by a mission to enhance citizens' capacity to hold public institutions accountable. Since its informal beginnings in Jamie Kalven's reporting in the early 2000s, it has addressed patterns of neglect and abuse by public institutions, advancing themes of visibility and place in the urban environment through human rights documentation, investigative reporting, and civil rights litigation.

Rafah: Black Friday, 2015. Videos, photographs, and 3-D model. Commissioned by Amnesty International

THE FUNAMBULIST
Established 2015, Paris

The Funambulist is a print and online magazine dedicated to the politics of space and bodies. Every two months it proposes spatial perspectives on political, anticolonial, antiracist, queer, feminist, and/or anti-ableist struggles. It was initiated as an editorial project of the existing Funambulist blog and podcast. The production team currently comprises Léopold Lambert, Nadia El Hakim, Margarida Nzuzi Waco, and Carol Que. Lambert is a trained architect, a writer, and the founding editor of the Funambulist; his research focuses on the examination of the political violence enacted by architecture as the discipline that organizes bodies in space. El Hakim is an architect and exhibition designer researching mutations of the design process in the context of economic and political crisis in Europe and the Middle East. Waco is a business strategist mediating the intersection of publishing and architecture. Que is the magazine's copy editor as well as a writer, researcher, and educator. The Funambulist has received four Graham Foundation grants.

Cover of *The Funambulist* 13 (September–October 2017)

MARIA GASPAR
Born 1980, Chicago;
lives and works in Chicago

In the hands of Maria Gaspar, sculpture, sound, performance, and installation are more than artistic mediums—they are tools for investigating "the politics of location." An interdisciplinary artist based in Chicago, Gaspar uncovers and challenges traditional power dynamics, addressing what she calls "spatial justice" by exposing systemic imbalances and making visible those whose voices are often marginalized or silenced. She works in sites overlooked by history, employing an arsenal of creative tactics that vary in scale and duration, with the ultimate goal of liberation—for oppressed groups and neglected locales. Her recent projects include site-responsive interventions related to Chicago's Cook County Jail. Gaspar is a recipient of the Imagining Justice Award from the Art for Justice Fund, a Robert Rauschenberg Artist as Activist Fellowship, a Creative Capital Award, and a Joan Mitchell Emerging Artist Grant. She is an assistant professor at the School of the Art Institute of Chicago.

THEASTER GATES
Born 1973, Chicago;
lives and works in Chicago

Theaster Gates's work utilizes sculpture and performance to explore space theory and land development. Drawing on his interest and training in urban planning and preservation, Gates redeems spaces that have been left behind, upturning art values, land values, and human values. In all aspects of his work, he contends with the notion of black space as a formal exercise—one defined by collective desire, artistic agency, and the tactics of a pragmatist. Gates has exhibited and performed at Sprengel Museum, Hannover, Germany (2018); Kunstmuseum Basel (2018); National Gallery of Art, Washington, DC (2017); Fondazione Prada, Milan (2016); Whitechapel Gallery, London (2013); *Documenta 13* (2012); Gropius Bau, Berlin (2019); and Palais de Tokyo, Paris (2019). He was awarded the Légion d'Honneur in 2017 and has also received the Artes Mundi 6 prize, the Nasher Prize for Sculpture, and the Urban Land Institute J. C. Nichols Prize for Visionaries in Urban Development.

Screening as part of *Radioactive: Stories from Beyond the Wall*, Cook County Jail, Chicago, 2018

Stony Island Arts Bank, Chicago, an abandoned 1920s bank turned arts space restored by Rebuild Foundation, led by Theaster Gates. Photo: Tom Harris; © Hedrich Blessing, courtesy Rebuild Foundation

JORGE GONZÁLEZ
Born 1981, Boriquén (Puerto Rico);
lives and works in Boriquén

Jorge González's artistic practice serves as a platform for the recuperation of Boricua material culture, in an attempt to create new narratives between the indigenous and the modern. In 2014, he founded Escuela de Oficios in response to omissions of dominant histories and deteriorating academic spaces. Proposing recovery through community regeneration, Escuela de Oficios creates spaces for collective learning and promotes self-directed education. Its activities include mapping, documenting and employing artisanal techniques, and creating a mobile program that includes conversations, workshops, and exhibitions. His work has been exhibited internationally, including solo presentations at Embajada, San Juan; International Studio and Curatorial Program, New York; and Roberto Paradise, San Juan. His work also has been included in exhibitions at Los Angeles Contemporary Exhibitions and the Whitney Museum of American Art, New York, and in *Documenta 14*. In 2017, González was awarded the Davidoff Arts Initiative grant to be part of Escuela Flora in Bogotá.

The Garden, 2018

Escuela de Oficios: Visit to Guadalupe Villalobos's furniture workshop with craft promoter Robinson Rosado, Barrio Cordillera, Ciales, Puerto Rico, 2016. Photo: Max Toro

OLA HASSANAIN
Born 1985, Khartoum, Sudan;
lives and works in Khartoum
and Utrecht, Netherlands

Early in her architecture career, Ola Hassanain developed a growing sense of frustration over the gulf between architectural theory and the real-world actualities of the built environment. As she pursued advanced degrees, she trained her focus on the subtle politics of space— namely, how built spaces react to and reinforce gender roles and stereotypes. When her family scattered across the globe due to economic collapse in Sudan, her fascination with the ways the built environment reflects, responds to, and shapes the lives of those who inhabit it increased. Her most recent work explores the idea of "space as discourse," an expanded notion of space that encompasses political and environmental questions. Hassanain's honors include the University of Westminster's Quintin Hogg Trust scholarship, a BAK—basis voor actuele kunst fellowship, and a Prince Claus Fund for Culture and Development grant. She is currently a PhD candidate at the Academy of Fine Arts, Vienna.

WALTER J. HOOD
Born 1958, Charlotte, North Carolina;
lives and works in Oakland, California

Artist, designer, and educator Walter J. Hood founded Hood Design Studio in Oakland, California, in 1992. Believing that everyone needs beauty in their lives, he makes use of everyday objects for landscape design and public sculpture that generate new apertures through which to see the emergent beauty, strangeness, and idiosyncrasies of urban space. His firm's nationally recognized projects include the de Young Museum gardens in San Francisco's Golden Gate Park; the Broad Museum Plaza, Los Angeles; and the Arthur Ross Terrace and Garden at the Cooper Hewitt, Smithsonian Design Museum, New York. The studio has received numerous honors, including the American Institute of Architects (AIA) Award for Collaborative Achievement and the Cooper Hewitt National Design Award in Landscape Design. In addition to serving as creative director of his eponymous firm, Hood is professor of landscape architecture, environmental planning, and urban design at the University of California, Berkeley.

Broad Plaza, The Broad museum, Los Angeles, 2015.
Photo: Mike Boster, courtesy the Broad Foundation

KELEKETLA! LIBRARY
Established 2008, Johannesburg

Keleketla! Library engages with multifaceted cultural presentations: literary, film, music, visual art, and other, still undefined forms. *Keleketla* is a Sepedi word said at the beginning of a story, in response to the storyteller's "once upon a time." It is an acknowledgment: "I am here, willing to listen to your story with active participation." This expression of active listening reflects the mission of Keleketla! Library, founded by Rangoato Hlasane and Malose Malahlela in Johannesburg in 2008. Nominated for the Vera List Center Prize for Art and Politics (2014) and the Visible Award (2017), Keleketla! Library participated in the 10th Berlin Biennale for Contemporary Art (2018) and has been working across Africa and beyond as a member of Another Roadmap for Arts Education's Africa Cluster.

Malose Malahlela, *FM*, 2014. Site-specific sound installation for the underground shooting range below Drill Hall Precinct, Johannesburg. Photo: Eric Dube

AVIJIT MUKUL KISHORE AND ROHAN SHIVKUMAR
Born 1969, Lucknow, India; lives and works in Mumbai
Born 1971, Hyderabad, India; lives and works in Mumbai

Avijit Mukul Kishore and Rohan Shivkumar's shared passions for film and architecture rendered them natural collaborators. Kishore is a filmmaker and cinematographer who stretches the boundaries of documentary filmmaking, incorporating multidisciplinary elements as he explores the capacity and influence of moving images. Shivkumar is an urban designer and architect interested in the social issues that shape usage of and infrastructure around built spaces. As collaborators the pair have delved into an exploration of Indian modernity that encompasses a look at the country's changing citizenry and evolving ideas about how architecture defines notions of home, spotlighted in their recent film *Nostalgia for the Future*, which screened at *Documenta 14* (2017). Kishore has directed nearly a dozen films and worked as a cinematographer on more than thirty. Shivkumar has served as principal of his own architecture and interior design firm since 2002. Both men have deep roots in academia, regularly giving lectures, publishing articles, and curating film programs.

Avijit Mukul Kishore, *Vertical City*, 2010 (still)

TANYA LUKIN LINKLATER AND TIFFANY SHAW-COLLINGE
Born 1976, Kodiak, Alaska;
lives and works in North Bay,
Ontario, Canada
Born 1982, Calgary, Alberta, Canada;
lives and works in Edmonton, Alberta

With roots in Indigenous communities of southern Alaska and central Alberta, respectively, the artist Tanya Lukin Linklater and the architect and artist Tiffany Shaw-Collinge share relational networks, intellectual concerns, and long-standing interests in Indigenous materials and forms. These shared concerns ground their conversations and collaboration. Lukin Linklater frequently employs performances, videos, and installations to call attention to overlooked histories—an effort that she renders all the more affecting by her choice of venues: often museums with collections that include Indigenous belongings (sometimes called artifacts). Shaw-Collinge similarly draws on interdisciplinary interests in her practice, working as an artist, curator, and architect and probing layered meanings through her materials and design choices. Among their recent honors, Lukin Linklater was the inaugural recipient of Canadian Art's Wanda Koop Research Fund, and Shaw-Collinge was commissioned to create public artworks for Edmonton's Indigenous Art Park, Winnipeg's Markham bus station, and Kinistinâw Park in Edmonton.

Tanya Lukin Linklater, *Horse Hair Question 1 (in three parts)*, 2016. Photo: Blaine Campbell

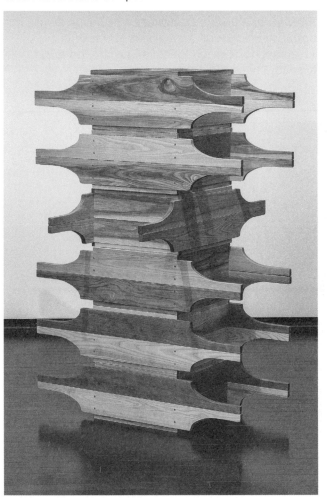

MASS DESIGN GROUP
Established 2008, Kigali, Rwanda;
Boston; and Poughkeepsie, New York

MASS, or Model of Architecture Serving Society, began with the design and construction of the Butaro District Hospital in Rwanda, a project of Partners in Health and the Rwandan Ministry of Health. The partnership evolved into a nonprofit architecture and design collective that works to advance justice, promote dignity, and improve human and community health through mission-driven design processes. Understanding that architecture is never neutral, MASS leverages design to improve the human and physical systems necessary for health, justice, and equity. Its practice strives to demonstrate that great design can engage civic responsibility, deliver economic and social outcomes, and inspire by bringing beauty and dignity to those most often denied or displaced by architecture. Among MASS's critically acclaimed projects are the National Memorial for Peace and Justice in Montgomery, Alabama; the Kigali Genocide Memorial in Rwanda; and *The Embrace*, a public sculpture in Boston made in collaboration with the artist Hank Willis Thomas, honoring Coretta Scott King and Martin Luther King Jr.

National Memorial for Peace and Justice, Montgomery, Alabama, 2018. Photo: Alan Ricks

VINCENT MEESSEN
Born 1971, Baltimore;
lives and works in Brussels

A visual artist working on the fringe of curatorship, Vincent Meessen does not limit the mediums in his artistic arsenal. He gravitates toward narratives teased out of history, calling on assorted ephemera, objects, and environments to expose parallels and associations among seemingly disparate places and events. His projects trace and upend the West's influence on the documentation of historical events and movements, challenging accepted tenets and stirring controversy as a means of initiating both introspection and public dialogue. A member of the artistic research and production platform Jubilee, Meessen embraces the subjugation of the individual auteur and celebrates the intellectual prowess of collectives. He has presented films and artworks in museums around the world, including a recent solo show at Centre Pompidou, Paris, and he has participated in the Venice, Shanghai, and Taipei biennials, among other exhibitions.

SIISIS, 2015. Photo: Philippe De Gobert

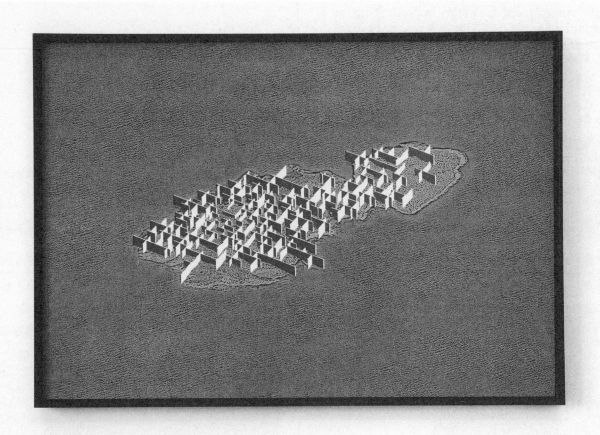

MOVIMENTO SEM TETO DO CENTRO (CITY CENTER HOMELESS PEOPLE'S MOVEMENT) IN COLLABORATION WITH ESCOLA DA CIDADE AND O GRUPO INTEIRO
Established 2000, São Paulo
Established 2014, São Paulo
Established 1996, São Paulo

Founded on the belief that workers must have access to housing, Movimento Sem Teto do Centro (MSTC) fights on behalf of families experiencing homelessness. Led by Carmen Silva—an activist, immigrant, and mother who has herself experienced homelessness—the organization promotes debate and activism around structural failures of urban planning and housing policies, helping citizens gain access to affordable homes. Through MSTC's actions, over dozen previously abandoned or unoccupied buildings in São Paulo are now inhabited by people in need. MSTC partners with architects, artists, independent media groups, universities, and cultural and recreational institutions to integrate the population it serves into the cultural and civic fabric of São Paulo. Its partners include O Grupo Inteiro, an interdisciplinary collective that combines architecture, graphic design, and curating, and Associação Escola da Cidade, a teachers-run design school located in downtown São Paulo that offers undergraduate degrees in architecture and urbanism.

The 9 de Julho occupation, São Paulo, 2018.
Photo: Carolina Vega

JOAR NANGO
Born 1979, Áltá, Norway

Joar Nango works with site-specific installations and self-made publications that explore the boundary between architecture, design, and visual art. Thematically speaking, his work relates to questions of Indigenous identity, often through investigating oppositions and contradictions in contemporary architecture. Nango has explored modern Sámi spaces through a self-published zine series entitled *Sámi Huksendáidda: the FANzine*, the design project Sámi Shelters, and the mixtape/clothing project Land & Language. He is a founding member of the architecture collective FFB, which works with temporary installations in urban contexts. Nango's works have been exhibited in *Documenta 14*, as well as at 161 Gallon Gallery and Gallery Deluxe Gallery in Halifax, Galerie SAW Gallery in Ottawa, and at Western Front in Vancouver. He is currently involved in setting up a network of Sámi architects across Sápmi through the ongoing Indigenous architecture lab Girjegumpi.

Pitch Black, 2016. Installation for the Art Ii Biennale of Northern Environmental Sculpture Art, Ii, Finland

PALESTINE HEIRLOOM SEED LIBRARY
Established 2014, Bethlehem

Founded by Vivien Sansour, the Palestine Heirloom Seed Library is an initiative that seeks to preserve and promote heritage and threatened seed varieties, traditional Palestinian farming practices, and the cultural stories and identities associated with them. Based in the village of Battir, a UNESCO World Heritage site outside Bethlehem, the library also serves as a space for collaborations with artists, poets, writers, journalists, and other members to showcase and promote their talents and work. Working closely with farmers, Sansour has identified key seed varieties and food crops that are threatened with extinction and would provide the best opportunities to inspire local farmers and community members to actively preserve their bioculture and recuperate their local landscape. The library also has launched a global platform for conversations about biocultural heritage. Its Traveling Kitchen is a mobile venue for social engagement in different communities, promoting cultural preservation through food choices.

ALEXANDRA PIRICI
Born 1982, Bucharest;
lives and works in Bucharest

Alexandra Pirici has cultivated a boundary-defying artistic practice that fuses dance, sculpture, spoken word, music, and performance. She choreographs ongoing actions, blurring the distinction between performer and audience. Her projects often explore site-specific histories, institutional hierarchies, the presence and limits of the body, and the function of gesture in art. Her work has been exhibited internationally, including at the New Museum, New York; Centre Pompidou, Paris; Museum Ludwig, Cologne; State Russian Museum, Saint Petersburg; Neuer Berliner Kunstverein; Tate Modern, London; Museum of Modern Art, Warsaw; and Van Abbemuseum, Eindhoven, among many others. She has also participated in Skulptur Projekte Münster, the Venice Biennale, Manifesta 10, and the 9th Berlin Biennale.

If You Don't Want Us, We Want You, 2011. Performance at the Equestrian Statue of Carol I, or the Monument to the 1989 Revolution, Bucharest, Romania

Seed notes, n.d. Courtesy Vivien Sansour

RAUMLABOR
Established 1999, Berlin

Formed in response to the rapid and unrestrained development of Berlin after the fall of the Berlin Wall, Raumlabor—whose name translates to "space laboratory"—sees the role of an architect as that of a negotiator who highlights social problems rather than solving them. This collective of nine practitioners works at the intersection of architecture, city planning, public art, and intervention, often proposing playful, temporary or speculative "urban prototypes" aimed at transforming the built landscape. Examples have included pneumatic structures, submarines made of waste materials, and a mountain built from the rubble produced by uncovering a buried canal. Members often respond to sites that are abandoned, leftover, or in transition; their approach is used to both critique and influence official city planning processes. The group's recent honors include the Global Award for Sustainable Architecture, the Curry Stone Design Prize, and the Core77 Design Award.

Public sauna, Gothenburg, Sweden, 2014

RIWAQ
(CENTER FOR ARCHITECTURAL CONSERVATION)
Established 1991, Ramallah, Palestine

A nongovernmental organization, Riwaq develops alternative architectural practices with the goal of cultivating social change. Founded by architect and writer Suad Amiry, and co-directed by Dr. Khaldun Bshara and Shatha Safi, Riwaq has a multidisciplinary, majority-women team. It sees the protection of historic sites as key to the reinterpretation of fragmented landscapes, and as a strategy for the recovery of precolonial identities and memories. Working among architecture, art, and spatial design, Riwaq employs speculative ideas as a means to imagine possibilities for healing a wounded land and reclaiming space. In close collaboration with rural communities in occupied Palestine, Riwaq has shifted the paradigm of architectural conservation toward a multidisciplinary approach that accounts for personal and historical narratives, environmental factors, socioeconomic conditions, and cultural identities. Its honors include the Aga Khan Award for Architecture, the Curry Stone Design Prize, the Prince Claus Award, and the Habitat for the Best Worldwide Architectural Practices.

Abwein, Palestine, 2011. Photo: Lana Judeh

RMA ARCHITECTS
Established 1990, Mumbai and Boston

RMA Architects was founded by Rahul Mehrotra, a practicing architect, urban designer, and educator, to execute projects for government and nongovernmental agencies, corporate interests, and private individuals and institutions, with a commitment to advocacy in the city of Mumbai. Mehrotra is a professor of urban design and planning at the Harvard Graduate School of Design and has written and lectured extensively on architecture, conservation, and urban planning in India. In 2018 RMA Architects received a special mention at the Venice Biennale of Architecture for three projects addressing issues of intimacy and empathy, social boundaries, and hierarchies. Since 2014 Mehrotra has been a member of the International Committee of Architecture Critics. His latest publication is *Taj Mahal: Multiple Narratives* (2017), coauthored with Baig Amita. RMA Architects' work has earned a RIBA International Fellowship, the 2019 J. Irwin and Xenia S. Miller Prize, and the Cooper-Hewitt National Design Award, among other honors.

KMC Corporate Office, Hyderabad, India, 2012. Photo: Carlos Chen

JIMMY ROBERT
Born 1975, Saint-Claude, Guadeloupe, France

Jimmy Robert's practice encompasses performance, photography, film, video, and drawing, frequently collapsing distinctions between these mediums. Using photography as a starting point for his works on paper, Robert blurs the divisions between two and three dimensions, as well as between image and object. This interest in blurred boundaries integrates his performative work—which includes choreographed elements in the context of an exhibition or in relationship to architecture—with his larger practice. In previous works he has explored the politics of spectatorship by reworking seminal avant-garde performances in ways that complicate their racial and gendered readings. Robert's work has been featured in a solo exhibition at the Museum of Contemporary Art Chicago, in commissions by *Performa 17* and the Glass House, in performances at New York's Museum of Modern Art, at the Berlin and Dakar biennials, and in a Satellite presentation organized by the Jeu de Paume, Paris.

Imitation of Lives, 2017. Performance for *Performa 17*. Courtesy Performa and The Glass House. Photo: Michael Biondo

SETTLER COLONIAL CITY PROJECT AND AMERICAN INDIAN CENTER OF CHICAGO
Established 2019, Ann Arbor, Michigan, and Guayaquil, Ecuador
Established 1953, Chicago

The Settler Colonial City Project is a research collective that considers cities in the Americas as spaces of ongoing colonialism and Indigenous survival. Cofounded by Andrew Herscher and Ana María León, the project aims to engage, document, circulate, and activate conjoined Indigenous and settler colonial urban histories and their contemporary manifestations. Herscher and León are also two of the cofounders of Detroit Resists, a coalition of activists, artists, and architects working on behalf of an inclusive, equitable, and democratic city. They work individually within a series of other militant research groups, including We the People of Detroit Community Research Collective and the Decolonizing Pedagogies Workshop. As part of the 2019 Chicago Architecture Biennial, the Settler Colonial City Project is collaborating with the American Indian Center of Chicago (AIC). The oldest urban-based Native membership community center in the United States, AIC strives to be the primary cultural and community resource for Native Americans in the Chicago metropolitan area, offering academic, healthcare, and social service programs.

Detroit Resists, Digital Occupation of the US Pavilion at the Venice Biennale of Architecture. 2016. Photo: Detroit Resists

SOMATIC COLLABORATIVE
Established 2008, New York

Somatic Collaborative is a research-based design practice focusing on a speculative approach to architecture, landscape, and urbanism, engaging a diverse set of spatial contexts and design procedures. Its multidimensional approach encompasses projects ranging from interior furnishings to open territories, using architectural commissions, design competitions, and applied research to facilitate inventive construction of space. Founder and managing partner Felipe Correa is the Vincent and Eleanor Shea Professor and Chair of the Department of Architecture at the University of Virginia and co-director of the South America Project, a transcontinental applied research network that endorses the role of design within rapidly transforming geographies of South America. A Somatic collaborator since 2015, Devin Dobrowolski draws on his experience in architecture, landscape architecture, and art to work at the confluence of large-scale data visualization and material fabrication, focusing on the broader sociopolitical dynamics of materials in the context of global production chains. Somatic's outreach includes projects in Brazil, Ecuador, Germany, Mexico, South Korea, and the United States.

Bird's-eye view of the network of hydroelectric dams along the lower Paraná River in relation to the major urban corridor along the coast linking São Paulo and Rio de Janeiro, 2018

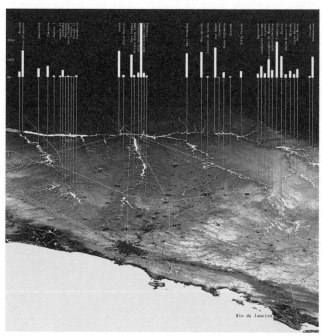

STUDIOBASAR
Established 2006, Bucharest

Reacting against Romania's history of privatization, distrust, and top-down decision-making in the realm of urban development, studioBASAR set out to empower a wide variety of people and practices in a quest for social transformation. Its founders, Alex Axinte and Cristi Borcan, saw architecture as a tool for effecting this transformation, providing a platform for collaboration among communities and creative professionals in questioning existing uses of public and private space and proposing new ones. Its strategies include collaborative design and production, research by design, placemaking activities, civic pedagogy, and creative reuse of existing structures. The studio's ultimate goal is the creation of cities that are more collaborative, accessible, and just. Among its recent honors, studioBASAR was recognized as a finalist for the 2014 European Prize for Urban Public Space, and it received the 2018 Romanian National Cultural Fund Award for "cultural activation in relation to the public space."

Public Bath, 2012. Temporary installation for the Street Delivery #7 festival, Bucharest

DO HO SUH
Born 1962, Seoul;
lives and works in London

Do Ho Suh's sculptural installations and impermanent structures begin with the ways his own peripatetic existence emblematizes global mobility. Often constructed of stitched polyester fabric and steel, his works materialize memories of the interiors of his former homes. These ghostlike, monochromatic installations appear to float, upending the density and permanence typically associated with built architecture. Designed as modular objects that can be folded and packed into a suitcase, the works address transience and displacement through manipulation of material. His own body in motion, moving across the globe as he travels and inhabits different cities, links disparate geographies; his sculptures evoke questions of belonging and cultural specificity in a global culture, and resonances between built and psychic interior spaces. Suh's work is in museum collections worldwide, including the Museum of Modern Art, New York; Tate, London; National Museum of Modern and Contemporary Art, Seoul; and Mori Art Museum, Tokyo.

Robin Hood Gardens, Woolmore Street, London E14 0HG,
2018 (still). Courtesy the artist; Lehmann Maupin, New York, Hong Kong, and Seoul; and Victoria Miro, London / Venice

SWEET WATER FOUNDATION
Established 2009, Chicago

Sweet Water Foundation (SWF) is an emerging community land trust in the heart of Chicago's South Side. SWF utilizes a blend of urban agriculture, art, and education to transform vacant spaces and abandoned buildings into economically and ecologically productive and sustainable community assets. It is rooted in the holistic practice of regenerative neighborhood development, an interdisciplinary social justice method that creates safe and inspiring spaces while cultivating healthy, intergenerational communities and transforming the ecologies of once "blighted" neighborhoods. Its projects engage youth, skilled workers, and artists to produce locally grown food and build affordable housing. SWF's Perry Avenue Commons site has become a model of sustainable, twenty-first-century community development, attracting thousands of locals and visitors annually. The organization's work has received an ArtPlace America National Creative Placemaking Award and an Environmental STEM Award from Underwriters Laboratories and the North American Association for Environmental Education for its multifaceted development at the Commons.

TERRITORIAL AGENCY
Established 2007, London

Established by the architects and urbanists John Palmesino and Ann-Sofi Rönnskog, Territorial Agency combines architecture, analysis, advocacy, and action for integrated spatial transformations of contemporary territories. The organization works to strengthen the capacity of local and international communities for comprehensive spatial transformation in the Anthropocene, a geologic epoch shaped by human impacts. Its activities are grounded in extensive territorial analysis, with a focus on complex remote sensing representations that monitor the transformations of physical structures in inhabited territories. Territorial Agency's work has appeared at HKW Haus der Kulturen der Welt, Berlin; ZKM Karlsruhe; BAK Utrecht; Tate Modern; Serpentine Galleries; the Venice Biennale; and the Musée d'Art Moderne, Paris. Palmesino and Rönnskog are unit masters at the Architectural Association, London. Palmesino is a founding member of multiplicity, an international research network based in Milan, and Rönnskog is a research fellow at the Oslo School of Architecture and Design. They led the research of ETH Zurich / Studio Basel Contemporary City Institute.

Thought Barn, 2017. Ongoing installation

Anthropocene Observatory: Multibeam sonar bathymetric model of the continental shelf off the coast of Nova Scotia, 2013

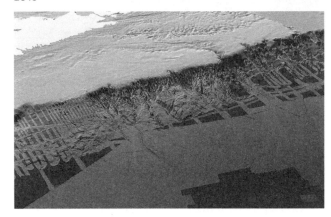

OSCAR TUAZON
Born 1975, Seattle;
lives and works in Los Angeles

Oscar Tuazon is an interdisciplinary artist who uses natural and industrial materials to create sculptures and installations that refer to minimalist sculpture, extreme do-it-yourself aesthetics, and vernacular architecture. Drawing on his long-standing interest in how the built environment is redefined through the act of inhabitation, Tuazon frequently uses wood, concrete, glass, steel, light fixtures, and piping to create his structures and installations, responding directly to the sites in which they are presented. Tuazon's approach is informed by his training in architecture, urban studies, and studio art from the Whitney Museum of American Art Independent Study Program and Cooper Union School of Architecture, both in New York. His work has been exhibited widely across the United States and Europe, with recent solo presentations at the Eli and Edythe Broad Art Museum at Michigan State University, East Lansing; Luhring Augustine, New York; Skulptur Projekte Münster; Galerie Eva Presenhuber, Zurich; Hammer Museum, Los Angeles; and Place Vendôme, Paris.

Installation view of *Oscar Tuazon: Water School* at the Eli and Edythe Broad Art Museum at Michigan State University, East Lansing, 2019. Photo: Eat Pomegranate Photography

USINA-CTAH
Established 1990, São Paulo

Usina-CTAH is an association of professionals who collaborate with community-led dwelling movements across São Paulo and throughout Brazil in the struggle for land and housing access. Over the past decade the country has undergone an intense period of democractic reconstruction after more than twenty years of military dictatorship. In this spirit Usina-CTAH joins professional expertise with political action and advocacy, engaging architecture, construction, and building technology as fields in which to explore new models of production and worker participation. Usina-CTAH believes that every action is informed by both technical and political conditions. The group therefore utilizes the skills of its members to guide and professionalize the efforts of those who traditionally are excluded from decision-making around policy and planning. In 2015 Usina-CTAH was named Architect and Urbanist of the Year by the National Brazilian Federation of Architects. Most recently, the group has participated in the Lisbon Architecture Triennial, the Panamerican Architecture Biennial of Quito, and the International Architecture Biennial of São Paulo.

WENDELIEN VAN OLDENBORGH
Born 1962, Rotterdam; lives and works in Rotterdam and Berlin

Wendelien van Oldenborgh uses the cinematic format as a methodology for production and as the basic language for various forms of presentation. Her work often involves public shoots that capture interactions between individuals in locations that invoke political and historical themes. In the process, she collaborates with participants to guide the work to its final outcome. Recently, her practice has been informed by research on the subjects of colonialism and cultural difference, social struggle, and modernity—issues embedded in the structures of our environment. Van Oldenborgh has exhibited in the Venice, Cuenca, São Paulo, and Istanbul biennials, and her work is represented in museum collections throughout Europe. She is a winner of the Heineken Prize for Art, and since 2015 she has been a member of the Akademie van Kunsten in the Netherlands.

Future Footnotes, 2018. Installation view at Significant Other, Vienna

Construction view of COPROMO (Cooperativa Pró-Moradia de Osasco: Osasco Pro-Housing Cooperative), Osasco, Brazil, 1998

CLEMENS VON WEDEMEYER
Born 1974, Göttingen, Germany;
lives and works in Berlin

Clemens von Wedemeyer's video works use built space and multichannel installations to explore multiple viewpoints, story lines, points in time, and historical trajectories. The artist weaves together tropes of documentary and experimental film and uses composite imagery and gallery installations to materialize ideas about the contingency and constructedness of history and memory. Von Wedemeyer's artistic practice is research based, and he often animates historical narratives by filming at architectural sites. He draws from diverse historical subject matter and engages closely with art and film theory, frequently making reference to the history of film and theater in both the content and the form of his work. Von Wedemeyer's video installations often confront beholders in unexpected ways, dissolving the boundary between art and audience. His solo exhibitions have included installations at Neuer Berliner Kunstverein, Berlin; Museum of Contemporary Art, Chicago; MAXXI, Rome; and Paço das Artes, São Paulo.

Transformation Scenario, 2018. Video installation. Courtesy the artist; Gallery Jocelyn Wolff, Paris; and KOW Berlin

WOLFF ARCHITECTS
Established 2012, Cape Town, South Africa

Informed by the colonial history of their home in Cape Town, Heinrich and Ilze Wolff established their eponymous architecture firm as a vehicle for addressing social inequities as well as the erasure of indigenous landscapes and narratives. While spatial design is at the heart of its activities, the firm distinguishes itself through its reliance on a diverse set of employees and collaborators—including photographers, artists, filmmakers, and writers—and an expansive practice that encompasses social justice advocacy, research and scholarship, and conceptual art. Wolff bolsters its practical design business with consultancy services, an in-studio art gallery, a publication, and site-specific artistic interventions, all of which emphasize innovation and social engagement, blurring the lines between design, art, and activism. The firm's recent honors include a South African Institute of Architects National Award of Merit, a South African Property Owners' Association Innovation Award, and a Social Habitat prize at the Pan-American Architecture Biennial, Quito, Ecuador.

Installation view of *African Mobilities: this is not a refugee camp exhibition*, Architekturmuseum TUM, Munich, 2018

ZORKA WOLLNY
Born 1980, Krakow;
lives and works in Berlin

Zorka Wollny is an interdisciplinary artist who directs and choreographs performative works in collaboration with musicians, actors, dancers, and community members. Operating at the intersection of visual art, theater, activism, and contemporary music, her projects often explore the voice and body as tools of expression and public debate and respond directly to the histories and functions of specific architectural sites. She has staged performances in museums, factories, and empty buildings. Her works have been presented worldwide, including at De Appel, Amsterdam; Heroines of Sound Festival, Berlin; International Studio and Curatorial Program, New York; Edith-Russ-Haus für Medienkunst, Oldenburg, Germany; Institute of Contemporary Arts, London; Jazz and Experimental Music Festival, Istanbul; Akademie der Künste, Berlin; Galerie für Zeitgenössische Kunst, Leipzig; Savvy Contemporary, Berlin; Museum of Contemporary Art, Belgrade; Royal College of Art, London; and the 4th World Social Forum, Mumbai.

SANTIAGO X
Born 1982, Phoenix; lives and works in Chicago

Santiago X is a multidisciplinary artist who specializes in land art and architectural and new media installations. He is an enrolled member of the Coushatta Tribe of Louisiana (Koasati) and Indigenous Chamorro from the island of Guam (Hacha'Maori). His work explores human interaction with the built environment, history, technology, and constructed notions of order in a world of chaos. He often synthesizes old and new forms that test the boundaries between art and artifact. As a self-described Indigenous Futurist, he believes art can become something sacred that embodies life through a multiplicity of being. Currently, Santiago X is reinvigorating Indigenous mound building via two public earthwork installations along the Chicago and Des Plaines Rivers. This project marks the first time effigy earthworks will be constructed by Indigenous peoples in North America since the founding of the United States. Santiago X has exhibited internationally, including at Expo 2010 Shanghai, the Venice Biennale, and Ars Electronica in Linz, Austria.

Ophelias. Iconography of Madness, 2012. Performance at the Gdańsk Shakespeare Festival, Poland, 2013. Photo: Adam T. Burton

Aticintoloca (Man and The Black Snake), 2017. Installation and performance

PUBLICATION CONTRIBUTORS

YESOMI UMOLU is Director and Curator, Logan Center Exhibitions at the Reva and David Logan Center for the Arts, University of Chicago. Umolu directs a program of international contemporary art in the Logan Center Gallery and contributes to a number of strategic committees that drive the development of contemporary art, architecture, and urbanism on campus. She is a 2016 recipient of an Andy Warhol Foundation for the Visual Arts Curatorial Fellowship and recently served on the curatorial advisory board for the United States Pavilion at the 16th Venice Architecture Biennale.

SEPAKE ANGIAMA traverses the fields of art, architecture, performance, and writing. Her research project Her Imaginary addresses how science fiction and feminism may be harnessed to create a pedagogy of political and social imagination. Other projects include the programs and workshops School of Darkness; All good things must begin: A conversation between Audre Lorde and Octavia E. Butler; Reading Out Loud; The Mistress House; and We Summon All Beings Here Present, Past & Future, a public library of personal publications addressing radical black thought, modernism, and feminist theory. Angiama is the convener of Under the Mango Tree, a gathering of artist-run initiatives addressing the decolonization of education through embodied pedagogic practice.

PAULO TAVARES is an architect who lives in Brasília, where he is a professor at the Faculdade de Arquitetura e Urbanismo, University of Brasília. He has taught spatial and visual cultures at the School of Architecture, Design, and Arts at the Pontificia Universidad Catolica del Ecuador in Quito, and led the MA program at the Centre for Research Architecture at Goldsmiths, University of London. In 2017 he created the agency autonoma, a platform dedicated to urban research and intervention. Tavares is a long-term collaborator of Forensic Architecture, a multidisciplinary research group based at the University of London.

The AMERICAN INDIAN CENTER (AIC) was established in 1953 to help Native families cope with the transition from reservation to urban life following the selective termination of tribal status and the Indian relocation program of the 1950s. AIC strives to be the primary cultural and community resource for more than sixty-five thousand Native Americans in the Chicago metropolitan area, which is home to the third-largest urban Native American population, representing more than 125 tribal nations.

SHIBEN BANERJI is a historian of architecture and urbanism. His recent research situates Chicago architects Marion Mahony and Walter Burley Griffin amid a transnational group of artists, architects, pacifists, and anticolonial thinkers who turned to city design and development to shape a new democratic subject. Currently assistant professor of art history, theory, and criticism at the School of the Art Institute of Chicago, Banerji has served as a consultant to the World Bank and associate director of the Urban Design Research Institute, Mumbai. He holds a master's degree in city planning and a PhD in the history and theory of architecture from the Massachusetts Institute of Technology.

TIMUEL BLACK is a civil rights activist, educator, historian, US Army veteran, and community leader. As a political activist, Black helped establish the Congress of Racial Equality and the United Packinghouse Workers of America, among others. He was instrumental in the election of Chicago's first black mayor, Harold Washington, in 1983, as the pioneer of an independent, progressive black political movement, and was an adviser to a young Barack Obama in the 1980s. He is the author of *Bridges of Memory: Chicago's First Wave of Great Migration* (Northwestern University Press, 2005) and is professor emeritus of social sciences at the City Colleges of Chicago.

ADRIENNE BROWN is a literary scholar whose research focuses on American and African American cultural production in the twentieth century, with an emphasis on the history of perception as shaped by the built environment. She currently serves as associate professor of English at the University of Chicago, where she is affiliated with the Center for the Study of Race, Politics, and Culture and the Center for the Study of Gender and Sexuality. She is the author of *The Black Skyscraper: Architecture and the Perception of Race* (Johns Hopkins University Press, 2017) and co-editor of *Race and Real Estate* (Oxford University Press, 2015) with Valerie Smith.

DENISE FERREIRA DA SILVA writes on philosophy, political theory, feminist theory, law, and human rights. Her work focuses on how social scientific constructions of racial and cultural difference expose the violent basis and effects of modern onto-epistemological accounts and the ways they have constituted globality as an ethical-political field. She is the author of *Toward a Global Idea of Race* (University of Minnesota Press, 2007) and the co-editor (with Paula Chakravartty) of *Race, Empire, and the Crisis of the Subprime* (Johns Hopkins University Press, 2013). Ferreira da Silva is currently professor and director of the Social Justice Institute-GRSJ at the University of British Columbia.

MARIO GOODEN is a cultural practice architect and principal of Huff + Gooden Architects, New York. His practice engages the cultural landscape and the intersectionality of architecture, race, gender, sexuality, and technology. Gooden's work has been exhibited at the Venice Biennale of Architecture; the Netherlands Architecture Institute; the National Building Museum, Washington, DC; and the Municipal Arts Society, New York. Gooden is a Professor of Practice at the Graduate School of Architecture Planning and Preservation at Columbia University and is a co-director of the Global Africa Lab. He is a 2019 National Academy of Arts and Letters Award in Architecture recipient and the author of *Dark Space: Architecture, Representation, Black Identity* (Columbia University Press, 2016).

BRIAN HOLMES is an essayist, activist, and artist with a bent for political ecology. He holds a PhD in Romance languages from the University of California, Berkeley, has published scores of essays in English, French and Spanish, and has lectured at museums, universities, and alternative spaces across the world. In Chicago he collaborates with the Compass and Deep Time Chicago. His recent work in multimedia cartography can be found on his webpage, Ecotopia Today. He is now involved with the Haus der Kulturen der Welt and the Max Planck Institute in a large-scale territorial project entitled *The Mississippi: An Anthropocene River*.

EDUARDO KOHN studies the intimate relationships that the indigenous peoples of Ecuador's Upper Amazon have with one of Earth's most complex ecosystems. Focusing on how they understand and communicate with rain forest beings has led him to the audacious conclusion that complex living systems manifest "mind" in a variety of ways. From this he develops an empirically robust framework to understand our broader relationship to such mind-like phenomena with the goal of rethinking how to live in the face of unprecedented anthropogenic climate change. His prize-winning book *How Forests Think: Toward an Anthropology beyond the Human* (University of California Press, 2013) has been translated into seven languages. He teaches anthropology at McGill University in Montreal.

INAM KULA is an architect and activist based in Cape Town. She approaches urban planning and design in post-apartheid South Africa as an opportunity for integration and decolonization. Her work as a student and as an architect seeks to address the relationship between space and power and to confront uses of architecture that create and reinforce systems of marginalization and exclusion. She holds an honors degree in architecture from the University of Cape Town and is currently pursuing a master's in architecture. She also holds a postgraduate diploma in planning from the University of Witwatersrand, Johannnesburg.

LISA YUN LEE is a cultural activist and a scholar of art history, museum and exhibition studies, and gender studies whose research focuses on museums and diversity, cultural and environmental sustainability, and spaces that foster radically democratic practices. She currently serves as executive director of the National Public Housing Museum in Chicago and associate professor of public culture and museum studies at the University of Illinois at Chicago. She is the author of *Dialectics of the Body: Corporeality in the Philosophy of Theodor Adorno* (Routledge, 2004).

LESLEY LOKKO currently serves as director and professor of architecture of the Graduate School of Architecture, University of Johannesburg. An architect, academic, and novelist, her work engages with the intersections of identity, race, African urbanism, and the speculative nature of African architectural space. She is the editor of *White Papers, Black Marks: Race, Culture, Architecture* (University of Minnesota Press, 2000) and eleven bestselling novels. She serves frequently on international juries and is a BBC World contributor for Africa. In December 2019 Lokko will assume the role of dean of the Bernard and Anne Spitzer School of Architecture at The City College of New York.

JOHN N. LOW is a scholar of cultural history, American Indian studies, and religious studies. He is the author of *Imprints: The Pokagon Band of Potawatomi Indians and the City of Chicago* (Michigan State University Press, 2016). He is currently an associate professor of comparative studies at Ohio State University at Newark and as of September 2019, the director of the Newark Earthworks Center. A member of the Pokagon Band of Potawatomi Indians, his research and courses include American Indian histories, literatures, and communities, Native identities, American Indian religions, museums, material culture and representation, memory studies, and American Indian law and treaty rights.

AVIWE MANDYANDA is a scholar of urban planning and design based in Johannesburg. She holds a degree in urban planning and a masters in urban design from the University of Witwatersrand. She is a founding member of BlackStudio, a creative collective of young black urban planners, urban designers, and architects dedicated to conducting research, hosting public programs, and organizing exhibitions that explore the conceptualization and realization of black spatial imaginaries.

VIRGINIA DE MEDEIROS is a visual artist and educator whose audiovisual installations adapt documentary images to explore reality, subjectivity, and alterity. She participated in the 2006 and 2014 editions of the Bienal de São Paulo and was awarded the PIPA Prize (including the Popular Vote Exhibition) in 2015; 5th Marcantonio Vilaça Award for Fine Arts, Brazil; and Rede Nacional Funarte Artes Visuais 2009. Her work is part of a number of collections, including Associação Cultural Videobrasil, São Paulo; Centro Cultural São Paulo; Instituto Inhotim, Brumadinho, Brazil; and Museu de Arte do Rio, Rio de Janeiro.

EMMANUEL PRATT is an artist, designer, urban planner, educator, and scholar, and the cofounder of Sweet Water Foundation (SWF) in Chicago. He advocates for and actively cultivates healthy intergenerational communities that transform the urban ecology of so-called blighted spaces through a combined praxis of urban farming, architecture, art, and educational programming. Pratt has been an artist in residence at the Hyde Park Art Center, Chicago; an interpreter in residence at the Smart Museum of Art at the University of Chicago; and a Loeb Fellow at the Harvard Graduate School of Design. He has also served as the Charles Moore Visiting Lecturer at Taubman College of Architecture and Urban Planning at the University of Michigan.

TIM SAMUELSON is frequently referred to as Chicago's "walking encyclopedia." A historian of architecture and preservationist, Samuelson is the city's official cultural historian, serving in the Department of Cultural Affairs. He is also director of the Chicago Architectural Preservation Archive, an interactive resource for sharing architectural and historical materials. Previously, he worked with the Commission on Chicago Landmarks and as Curator of Architecture and Design at the Chicago Historical Society. He has organized a number of exhibitions at the Chicago Cultural Center that reflect his interests in both canonical architectural design and everyday buildings as integral to Chicago's history.

VIVIEN SANSOUR is an artist and conservationist who uses image, sketch, film, soil, seeds, and plants to enliven old cultural tales in contemporary presentations and to advocate for the protection of biodiversity as a cultural and political act. As the founder of Palestine Heirloom Seed Library and the Traveling Kitchen project, she works with farmers to promote seed conservation and crop diversity. She is co-director with Riad Bahour of the feature film El Bizreh Um El Fay, which was awarded best project at RamallahDoc 2015 and will be released in 2020. She has presented her work as an artist at the Jerusalem Fund Gallery, Washington, DC; SALT Art Center, Istanbul; and the 2019 Venice Biennale.

JENNIFER SCOTT is an anthropologist, curator, and public historian whose work explores connections between museums, art, place, and social justice. She currently serves as director and chief curator of Jane Addams Hull-House Museum at the University of Illinois at Chicago, leading the institution's exhibitions, community engagement efforts, and overall vision. Scott serves as a board member of the National Association for Museum Exhibition and as faculty in the graduate programs of Museum and Exhibition Studies at the University of Illinois at Chicago and the Art and Design History and Theory Program at The New School and Parsons School of Design in New York.

CARMEN SILVA leads the Movimento Sem Teto do Centro (City Center Homeless People's Movement), a social movement in São Paulo that works to advance housing rights for families and individuals living in vulnerable conditions. Silva's commitment to urban reform and social inclusion is rooted in her personal experience as an immigrant, mother, and social activist who has experienced homelessness. Her advocacy has included playing a leading role in Eliane Caffé's docu-fiction film from 2016, The Cambridge Squatter (originally titled Era o Hotel Cambridge), which tells the story of a group of families that transformed an abandoned building in downtown São Paulo into a public housing complex.

PELIN TAN is a researcher and writer working in the field of critical spatial practices, alternative pedagogies, and conflict territories. She studied sociology and completed her master's and PhD in art history with a focus on socially engaged art. Tan was a postdoctoral fellow in the MIT Program in Art, Culture and Technology (2011). She is a lead author of "Cities," in Rethinking Society for the 21st Century: Report of the International Panel on Social Progress (Cambridge University Press, 2018). Currently she is curator of the Gardentopia project of Matera 2019: European Capital of Culture, Italy, and a 2019–20 research fellow of the Center for Arts, Design and Social Research, Boston.

VINCENT TAO is a labor union organizer, housing activist, and educator whose work focuses on the history and practice of social movements. He previously served as education librarian at 221A in Vancouver, where he developed the institution's transdisciplinary research projects, community solidarity initiatives, and collaborative study programs.

ELIZABETH TODD-BRELAND is a scholar who specializes in twentieth-century US urban and social history, African American history, and the history of education. She currently serves as associate professor of history at the University of Illinois at Chicago and previously taught at Governors State University, University Park, Illinois, and the University of Chicago. Her book *A Political Education: Black Politics and Education Reform in Chicago since the 1960s* (University of North Carolina Press, 2018) was awarded the 2019 Pauli Murray Book Prize by the African American Intellectual History Society and the 2019 Outstanding Book Award by the American Educational Research Association.

CHEYANNE TURIONS is a curator and writer. Her work positions exhibitions and criticism as social gestures by which to respond to artistic practices by linking aesthetics and politics through discourse. Since 2008 she has been the co-director of No Reading After the Internet, a salon series concerned with understanding the act of reading aloud as its own media form. She has previously held positions at Art Metropole, the Art Museum at the University of Toronto, SBC galerie d'art contemporain, and the Vancouver Art Gallery. Currently turions is the curator at Simon Fraser University Galleries, Burnaby and Vancouver, and sits on the Board of Directors at 221A, Vancouver.

STEPHEN WILLATS is a conceptual artist whose work is situated at the intersection between art and disciplines including cybernetics, advertising systems research, learning theory, communications theory, and computer technology. Through multisensory installations that incorporate drawing, photography, audio, and film, he has developed a collaborative, interactive, and participatory practice grounded in the variables of social relationships and physical realities. His recent solo exhibitions have included presentations at the Middlesbrough Institute of Modern Art, England; Migros Museum of Contemporary Art, Zurich; Museo Tamayo Arte Contemporáneo, Mexico City; and Whitechapel Gallery, London. His work is included in many public collections, including at Tate Modern, London; National Portrait Gallery, London; and Henry Moore Institute, Leeds.

ACKNOWLEDGMENTS

The 2019 Chicago Architecture Biennial is the result of many collaborations, and we would like to acknowledge all those who have been part of this undertaking.

We are indebted to the entire Biennial staff for their hard work and dedication. Executive Director Todd Palmer and Deputy Director Rachel Kaplan were key partners at all stages. We recognize Tess Landon for her collaboration on learning initiatives, Christine Pundavela and Cathy Hsiao for managing press and marketing, Victoria Lynford for contributing to our fundraising efforts, and Jennifer Latshaw and Lauren McPhillips for managing events, public programs, and partnerships. Our curatorial work was strengthened by the tremendous efforts of our assistant curators, Marguerite Wynter and Alex Priest, who with good humor and pragmatism played crucial roles in shaping the Biennial's research initiatives, exhibition, programming, and publication. Curatorial Fellow Cecília Resende Santos also provided invaluable support. Our production team, led by Therese Marie Peskowits in partnership with James Lambrix, deftly shepherded the many Biennial contributors' projects from concept to realization. We thank Abby Chang for lending her drafting skills to our exhibition planning. We are also grateful to our external partners: Sara Griffin and the PR team at Camron, New York and London, for leading the Biennial's communications efforts; ELLA for developing a strong exhibition identity and a compelling design for this publication; Amanda Glesmann for providing essential publication management and oversight of our stellar editorial team; and PRODUCTORA for their partnership on the exhibition design.

We extend our thanks to the partners across the city who have made our offsite projects possible: Ghian Foreman and Paola Aguirre at the former Anthony Overton Elementary School and the residents of Bronzeville; Jaclyn Jacunski at the School of the Art Institute of Chicago; the Homan Square Community Advisory Board and the residents of North Lawndale; Jennifer Scott at the Jane Addams Hull-House Museum at the University of Illinois at Chicago; and Lisa Yun Lee at the National Public Housing Museum. For their collaboration on contributors' projects we also thank the American Indian Center, Jim Duignan and the team at Stockyard Institute, Site Design Group, Chicago Arts Partnerships in Education (CAPE), and Urban Juncture Boxville.

Sincere gratitude is due to the individuals, groups, and organizations who engaged with us during our research initiatives. We thank Robert Smith III, Jennifer Scott, and Emmanuel Pratt for lending a Chicago perspective to our travels. In São Paulo we benefited from the insights of Aparelha Luzia, Cafira Zoé, Camila Motta, Carla Caffé, Carmen Silva, Carol Tonetti, Cláudio Bueno, Coletivo PISA, Cristine Takuá, Érica Malunguinho, Escola da Cidade, Explode!, Giovanna Flumihan, O Grupo Inteiro, João Simões, Karoline Barros, Marian von Bodegraven, Marília Gallmeister, Movimento Sem Teto do Centro/Frente de Luta por Moradia (MSTC/FLM), Nelson da Cruz Souza, OUTROS—Laboratório para Outros Urbanismos, Patrícia Oliveira , Renato Cymbalista, and Teatro Oficina. Our time in Johannesburg was enriched by the perspectives of Lesley Lokko and the Graduate School of Architecture at the University of Johannesburg, Kemang Wa Lehulere, Ilze Wolff, Molemo Moiloa, Solam Mkhabela, Aviwe Mandyanda (BlackStudio), Inam Kula, Malose Malahlela, Rangoato Hlasane, MMA Design, Local Studio, Maker Valley Partnership, Fox Street Studios, and Thireshen Govender (Urban Works). In Vancouver we learned from 221A, Pollyanna 圖書館Library, Raymond Boisjoly, Fionn Byrne, Nathan Crompton, Dr. Dana Lepofsky, Margot Long, Lama Mugabo, Sara Stevens, Kwitsel Tatel, Vincent Tao, Ouri Scott, Urban Subjects, Alfred Waugh, T'uy't'anat Cease Wyss, School of Architecture + Landscape Architecture at the University of British Columbia, Courtenay Mayes, Jesse McKee,

Brian McBay, Patrick Condon, and Herb Varley and Meghan Harte.

The Chicago Architecture Biennial would not be possible without the continued support of city leadership. We are indebted to former mayor Rahm Emanuel for instituting the Biennial as a part of the city's cultural plan and for championing our work on this edition. We thank Mayor Lori Lightfoot for her support at this early stage of her tenure and are likewise grateful to Commissioner Mark Kelly and the City of Chicago's Department of Cultural Affairs and Special Events, who offered the Chicago Cultural Center as well as the staff expertise to help realize the Biennial. The board of the Chicago Architecture Biennial, chaired by Jack Guthman, have been outstanding advocates. Special thanks are due to Michelle Boone and Sarah Herda for their insights on the Biennial's curatorial development and to Lynn Lockwood for her work on fundraising.

To the Biennial contributors: thank you for your time, ideas, and creative energies. We extend our deepest gratitude to those who contributed to this publication, especially our lead essayists, Denise Ferreira da Silva, Eduardo Kohn, Lesley Lokko, and Pelin Tan.

We are grateful to our family and friends, who have supported us—in ways seen and unseen—throughout the course of this project.

Finally, this edition of the Chicago Architecture Biennial is inspired by the city of Chicago and its citizens. We are grateful for the opportunity to learn from this place and for the meaningful conversations we have had with Chicagoans about their city.

Yesomi Umolu, Sepake Angiama, and Paulo Tavares
2019 Chicago Architecture Biennial Curatorial Team

CHAIRMAN'S STATEMENT

The Chicago Architecture Biennial welcomes a wide audience: architecture and design professionals, whose response to previous iterations has led to international acclaim within the field; Chicagoans from a variety of neighborhoods, who have propelled the Biennial to a respected place among our cultural institutions; and visitors who have included the exhibition among the attractions to see while in our city.

Graham Foundation Artistic Director Yesomi Umolu and her co-curators, Sepake Angiama and Paulo Tavares, have focused the exhibition on the intersection of architecture and the complex issues that challenge communities across the globe. They have applied their creative vision and engaged a talented, diverse team of architects, designers, planners, and critics in their exploration of those challenges. The exhibition and its related programs are both entertaining and thought-provoking, and I applaud the efforts of the curatorial team.

Even as it is intended to be an expression of Chicago's place in the international dialogue regarding architecture and the built environment, the Biennial is also a reflection of civic will. It is a product of former mayor Rahm Emanuel's Chicago Cultural Plan 2012. Throughout its as-yet-short history, Mayor Emanuel has been the Biennial's most ardent advocate. Mayor Lori Lightfoot is a staunch supporter; her enthusiasm for the Biennial is greatly appreciated. The city's Department of Cultural Affairs and Special Events has been, since the Biennial's inception, a valued partner.

Its relative youth notwithstanding, the Biennial has been embraced by many of Chicago's established cultural institutions, which have mounted exhibitions and programs that augment and amplify our mission. The association with the six anchor sites has expanded our visibility in neighborhoods across the city, as have our relationships with the Chicago Public Library and the Chicago Public Schools, the latter in tandem with the Chicago Architecture Center. We are grateful for our alignment with Expo Chicago and for the advice and support of its president and director, Tony Karman.

The Biennial's gifted board of directors has provided strong leadership to what only a few years ago was a start-up, not-for-profit enterprise. To each of them— Michelle Boone, Robert Clark, Keating Crown, Helyn D. Goldenberg, Valerie Corr Hanserd, Sarah Herda, Juan Gabriel Moreno, Lynn Lockwood Murphy, Mark P. Sexton, Robin Lowenberg Tebbe, Thomas Weeks, RaMona Westbrook, and Director Emeritus Ambassador Louis B. Susman—I extend my thanks for their support and guidance.

The staff of the Biennial, under the leadership of Todd Palmer and Rachel Kaplan, deserves special recognition and praise. Understaffed and overworked, their energy is endless and their dedication complete.

The Chicago Architecture Biennial would not have become a reality without the generous financial support of numerous individuals, foundations, and corporations. Founding Sponsor BP has again led the way. A list of all those whose contributions have been received as of this catalogue's printing may be found on page 211. We extend our thanks to all those whose largesse has permitted us to present the Biennial.

Finally, I thank our Biennial audience, who by visiting the exhibition or reading this catalogue bring to life our efforts to enage and understand the evolving social contexts of architecture in Chicago and beyond.

Jack Guthman
Chairman
Chicago Architecture Biennial

FOUNDING SPONSOR
BP

PRESENTING SPONSOR
Exelon

PRINCIPAL SPONSORS
Alphawood Foundation
Clayco

CREATING SPONSOR
Bluhm Family Charitable
  Foundation
Chicago Community Trust
Graham Foundation
Joe and Rika Mansueto
Lendlease
Zell Family Foundation

DESIGNING SPONSORS
Allstate Insurance Company
Choose Chicago
Loewenberg Charitable
  Foundation
Magellan Development Group
National Endowment for the Arts
John D. & Alexandra C. Nichols
  Family Foundation
The Revel Group
Taft Stettinius & Hollister LLP
Terra Foundation
Thornton Tomasetti
Walsh Foundation

SUPPORTING SPONSORS
Chicago Loop Alliance
Comcast
Crown Family Philanthropies
Joyce Foundation
John D. and Catherine T.
  MacArthur Foundation
Elizabeth Morse Charitable Trust
Ms. Sylvia Neil and Mr. Daniel
  Fischel
Polk Bros Foundation
Sara Szold

BLUEPRINT SPONSORS
Anne Kaplan
Jack & Sandra Guthman
Robert R. McCormick Foundation
Onni Group

FRIENDS
Helen Brach Foundation
Philip H. Corboy Foundation
Edlis-Neeson Foundation
Helyn Goldenberg and Michael
  Alper
Irving Harris Foundation
John H. Hart Foundation
Mellody Hobson and George
  Lucas
Mr. and Mrs. William L. Hood
Krueck + Sexton Architects
Metropolitan Pier and Exposition
  Authority
Neisser Family Foundation
Segal Family Foundation

BIENNIAL SOCIETY
Biennial Society Co-Chairs
David Cocagne
Eric T. McKissack
Biennial Society Members

Vickie Apostolopoulos
Sarah Brunstrum
Mary Dempsey
Eric Klinner
Dwayne MacEwen
Robin Malpass
Robert Mink
Benjamin Pardo
David W. Ruttenberg
Desiree Rogers
Jack Schwab
Tom Shapiro and Madeleine
  Grynsztejn
David Smykowski
Dia and Edward Weil
University of Illinois School of
  Architecture

PRESENTING PARTNER
City of Chicago, Department
  of Cultural Affairs and Special
  Events

**SIGNATURE EDUCATION
PARTNER**
Chicago Architecture
  Foundation

ALIGNING PARTNER
EXPO CHICAGO

PARTNER SITES
The 606 with the High Line
  Network
6018North
AIA Chicago
Alliance Française de Chicago
American Indian Center Chicago
Art Institute of Chicago
Beverly Arts Center
Bridgeport Art Center
Carrie Secrist Gallery
Chicago Architecture Center
Chicago Cultural Alliance
Chicago History Museum
Chicago Public Library
City of Chicago, Department of
  Planning and Development
The Danish Arts Foundation,
  Garfield Park Conservatory
  and Chicago Park District
DePaul Art Museum
The Richard H. Driehaus Museum
DuSable Museum of African
  American History
Elmhurst Art Museum
EXPO CHICAGO
Graham Foundation for Advanced
  Studies in the Fine Arts
Harris School of Public Policy
Hyde Park Art Center
Illinois Institute of Technology
  College of Architecture
Instituto Cervantes of Chicago
  and MAS Context
Jane Adams Hull House Museum
Logan Center for the Arts
Metropolitan Pier and Exposition
  Authority
Museum of Contemporary Art
  Chicago
National Museum of Mexican Art
National Museum of Puerto Rican
  Arts & Culture
National Public Housing Museum

Navy Pier, Inc.
Neubauer Collegium
The Night Gallery
The Renaissance Society at the
  University of Chicago
School of the Art Institute of
  Chicago
Skidmore, Owings & Merrill,
  McHugh Construction, Odico
  Formwork Robotics and
  Chicago Athletic Association
Smart Museum of Art
Swedish American Museum
Sweet Water Foundation
Tender House Project at the
  McCormick Bridgehouse &
  Chicago River Museum
University of Chicago
University of Illinois at Chicago
  School of Architecture
University of Illinois at Urbana-
  Champaign School of
  Architecture
Volume Gallery
Wrightwood 659

This listing reflects Biennial
sponsors and partners
confirmed as of July 12, 2019.

This listing represents all
contributors confirmed as of
July 12, 2019.

CREDITS

All images and reprint texts in this volume appear by permission of their creators and/or their representatives and the individuals named in the corresponding captions. Additional credits are specified below.

10–11: Courtesy Cornell University, PJ Mode Collection of Persuasive Cartography. 13–17: Fig. 1. Photo: Dennis Ha, 2019. Fig. 2. Photo: Carl Court/Getty Images, 2017. Fig. 3. Photo: Nic Bothma/EPA/Shutterstock, 2015. Fig. 4. Photo: Scott Olson/Getty Images, 2016. 22: Photo: Sebastián Hidalgo, 2018. Courtesy the photographer. 23–29: Fig. 1. Photo: Andrew Nelles/Reuters, 2015. Fig. 2. Photo: Nhlanhla Phillips/African News Agency, 2019. Fig. 3. Photo: Leo Correa/Associated Press, 2018. Fig. 4. Photo: Susanne Ure, 2012. Courtesy the photographer. Fig. 5. Photo: Jun Fujita, 1919. Courtesy the Chicago History Museum (ICHi-065477). 30–31: First printed in *The Atlantic* 313, no. 5 (June 2014): 55–71. Reprinted with permission from Tribune Content Agency. 40–41: Courtesy National Archives, College Park, MD, City Survey Files, Textual Records. 42–43: Photo: Bernard Kleina. Courtesy the photographer. 44–45: Courtesy Special Collections, University of Illinois at Chicago Library, Chicago Urban League records. 62: Courtesy Harboe Architects. 63–69: Fig. 1. Photo: Carol M. Highsmith/Buyenlarge/Getty Images. Fig. 2. Photo: Dean Hutton/Bloomberg/Getty Images, 2013. Fig. 3. Photo: Iwan Baan, 2006. Fig. 4. Photo: Cristina de Middel/Magnum Photos, 2011. Fig. 5. Paragon Group/NGAGE Media Zone. 70–71: Gwendolyn Brooks, *In The Mecca* (New York: Harper & Row, 1968), 4–5. Reprinted by consent of Brooks Permissions. 72–73: Photo: Charles Stewart, Jr. Courtesy Chicago History Museum (ICHi025338). 74: Photo: Paul D'Amato. Courtesy the photographer. 96: Photo: Cover Images/Associated Press. 97–103: Fig. 1. Photo: Eduardo Kohn, 2017. Fig. 2. Photo: Eduardo Kohn. Fig. 3. Photo: Eduardo Kohn, 2016. Fig. 4. Photo: Eduardo Kohn, 2017. Fig. 5. Photo: Pete Oxford/Minden Pictures, 2011. 104–5: Courtesy Archives of Michigan, General Photograph Collection. 107: First published in *Alaska Quarterly Review: Alaska Native Writers, Storytellers & Orators: The Expanded Edition* 17, nos. 3 and 4 (1999): 252, 253. Courtesy Susie Silook. 108: Courtesy National Archives, Washington, DC, Textual Records. Series: Indian Treaties, 1789–1869. Record Group 11: General Records of the United States Government, 1778–2006. 110: Courtesy Chicago History Museum, Albert F. Scharf Map Collection (ICHi-029629). 134: Photo: Charles Rex Arbogast/Associated Press. 135–40: Figs. 1–4. Courtesy City Plaza Collective. 141: Courtesy Chicago Public Library Special Collections and Preservation Division, Chicago Public Library Archives. 142–43: Courtesy Chicago History Museum, Coordinating Council of Community Organizations records, Small broadsides collection, Education: Chicago (ICHi-020839 and ICHi-020840). 152–53: First published in Michael J. Schaack, *Anarchy and Anarchists: A History of the Red Terror and the Social Revolution in America and Europe. Communism, Socialism, and Nihilism in Doctrine and in Deed. The Chicago Haymarket Conspiracy, and the Detection and Trial of the Conspirators* (Chicago: F.J. Schulte & Co., 1889). Courtesy University of Illinois at Urbana-Champaign Library, Illinois History and Lincoln Collection.

Image credits for the visual essays by Virginia de Medeiros, Mario Gooden, Vivien Sansour, and Stephen Willats appear on pages 59, 94, 131, and 167, respectively.

All images in the Featured Contributors section (pages 170–201) appear courtesy the contributors. Additional credits, where applicable, are noted in the image captions.

This book is published by the Chicago Architecture Biennial in association with Columbia Books on Architecture and the City on the occasion of the 2019 Biennial, *...and other such stories*, curated by Yesomi Umolu, Sepake Angiama, and Paulo Tavares and on view from September 19, 2019, through January 5, 2020.

Publication Manager:
Amanda Glesmann
Designers: ELLA
Production Designer:
James Brendan Williams
Assistant Curators: Alex Priest and Marguerite Wynter
Curatorial Fellow:
Cecília Resende Santos
Researcher:
Jessica D. Brier
Editors:
Karen Jacobson and Anne Ray
Proofreader: Carrie Wicks

Color separations by Echelon, Santa Monica

Printed and bound in Belgium by die Keure

Chicago Architecture Biennial
78 E. Washington Street
Chicago IL 60602
chicagoarchitecturebiennial.org

Columbia Books
on Architecture and the City
407 Avery Hall
1172 Amsterdam Ave
New York NY 10027
arch.columbia.edu/books

Distributed by
Columbia University Press
cup.columbia.edu

Library of Congress Control
Number: 2019944149
ISBN 978-1-941332-54-2

All images in this volume are reproduced by permission of the represented contributors and the photographers and/or owners named in the captions. Additional image credits appear on page 215.

Every reasonable effort has been made to credit copyright holders and to ensure the accuracy of the information presented herein. If errors or omissions are identified, please contact the Chicago Architecture Biennial so that corrections can be made in any subsequent edition.

The Chicago Architecture Biennial provides a platform for ground-breaking architectural projects and spatial experiments that demonstrate how creativity and innovation can radically transform our lived experience. Through its constellation of exhibitions, full-scale installations, and pro-gramming, the Biennial invites the public to engage with and think about architecture in new and unexpected ways, and to take part in a global discussion on the future of the field.